BAMTM
First Edition

Edited by David Ezekiel & Morgan Sharman

Contents

Accounting

Management

Marketing

BAMTM

BUSINESS - ACCOUNTING - MANAGEMENT - TALENT - MARKETING

B
BUSINESS

The importance of understanding effective business processes & mentalities that build a business that can last.

A
ACCOUNTING

The importance of understanding how to complete accountancy functions effectively for the business.

M
MANAGEMENT

Understanding the importance of processes used to complete the strategic & operational management activities effectively.

T
TALENT

Understanding the importance of supporting & leading teams that are extremely talented, while ensuring they maintain autonomy.

M
MARKETING

Understanding the importance of marketing tools & tactics and how they can define your business success.

Introduction

What is BAMTM - The Strategic Management System?

Welcome to the world of strategic management, where organisations thrive by skilfully planning, executing, and monitoring business goals and objectives. At its core, strategic management serves as a guiding framework, providing a structured approach that enables organisations to align their activities with their long-term vision and make well-informed decisions that contribute to ongoing success.

In this context, we are proud to present the BAMTM Strategic Management System—a valuable resource designed for strategic managers, equipping them with the necessary tools and knowledge to confidently tackle the challenges of the business world.

Whether it's setting and sticking to long-term goals or aligning teams with the business vision, BAMTM provides tried and tested approaches to management that ensure business success.

With BAMTM we delve into five critical business components—business management, accounting management, management approach, talent retention, and marketing. Recognising the crucial role these factors play in shaping business viability, we emphasise the importance of getting them right from the very beginning.

Introduction

With BAMTM, we guide you through a journey of understanding and implementation, providing strategies and actions that empower you as a strategic manager to build a solid foundation, that lays the groundwork for sustainable growth and long-term success.

Fostering unity: BAMTM was created based on the realisation that establishing a sustainable business in today's world goes beyond a hierarchical top-down approach. Instead, it requires an inclusive process where even the most junior team members grasp the importance of the company's goals and activities - and can contribute effectively to them.

Many of the management systems out there tend to prioritise senior management goal-setting and decision-making, often leaving junior team members uninformed and disconnected from the company's vision.

With BAMTM, we aim to foster collaboration and unity among all individuals in your business. It encompasses everyone, from strategic and operational managers to support staff and junior team members.

This approach acknowledges the importance of diverse perspectives, fostering ownership and motivation, enhancing communication and transparency, nurturing talent development, and building resilience in a rapidly changing business world.

Introduction

Finding and recruiting the right talent has become increasingly challenging, that's why BAMTM emphasises the importance of coaching and nurturing individuals within your team to become leaders and decision makers. By enabling each team member to actively contribute towards achieving the company's goals, you create a culture that empowers and motivates everyone.

Understanding the need to look ahead: For a strategic manager to create a culture of unity among managers and teams, it requires the ability to think long-term.

Understanding the importance of forward-thinking, BAMTM compels readers to consider the future of their business, as it is all too common for managers to prioritise the present moment, leading to decision-making that emphasises short-term gains at the expense of long-term sustainability.

It is crucial to recognise as a strategic manager, that the development of future products and productive teams demands a significant investment of your time in the present. Therefore, the strategic management process requires a proactive mindset to envision and plan for a clear and promising future.

With BAMTM, we offer step by step processes that can be implemented to safeguard the long-term success of the business.

Introduction

These processes are crafted to position the business for future prosperity, while also acknowledging the importance of maintaining consistent profitability. By integrating these practices, strategic managers can ensure the business thrives in the years to come.

BAMTM: The Strategic Management Guide For Owners, Directors and Senior Management

This book is the second instalment in the BAMTM series, building on the groundwork established by our initial book *BAMTM: The Operational Guide to Managing Your Business*, which primarily explored operational management activities.

In this guide, *BAMTM: The Strategic Management Guide For Owners, Directors and Senior Management*, we explore the pivotal role of business owners, to help you focus your attention on your role as a strategic manager and overcome challenges such as short-term thinking or micromanagement. Note – For simplicity, in the rest of the book we will mostly use the term *owners* to describe the following people:

- Owners
- Director
- Shareholders
- Person in significant control of a business
- Senior Management
- Strategic Management

Business

Working Out Profit

The pursuit of profitability is a fundamental objective that fuels growth and sustainability. Yet, discerning the genuine levels of profit necessary to achieve this goal requires an understanding of various factors. Profitability isn't a one-size-fits-all metric; it's influenced by industry dynamics, operational costs, market conditions, and long-term objectives.

To determine true profit levels, you must delve into cost analysis. Beyond the surface-level revenue, businesses must account for direct and indirect costs, fixed and variable expenses, and the often overlooked but critical factor of opportunity costs. An accurate grasp of these elements empowers decision-makers to set realistic revenue targets, allocate resources efficiently, and establish a solid foundation for sustainable profitability.

For businesses operating with low margins, the mission for profitability becomes a particularly arduous journey. These businesses grapple with razor-thin profit margins that leave little room for error or unexpected fluctuations. Achieving profitability in such contexts demands an unwavering commitment to cost control, operational efficiency, and strategic pricing.

The challenges are multifaceted. Maintaining competitiveness while managing costs requires a balance, as even minor deviations can impact the bottom line.

Business

Such endeavours demand inventory management, streamlined processes, and strategic partnerships to optimise supply chains.

For small businesses, the assessment of profitability becomes intricate. Limited resources, constrained budgets, and rapid market changes amplify the complexities of deciphering true profitability. The absence of sophisticated financial systems or dedicated departments can hinder the ability to analyse financial data comprehensively.

Moreover, small businesses often grapple with the challenge of balancing immediate cash flow needs with long-term profitability. Short-term survival pressures can sometimes lead to decisions that sacrifice long-term gains. This underscores the need for astute financial management, informed decision-making, and a holistic perspective that accounts for both short- and long-term objectives.

Businesses can adopt several strategies to enhance their chances of achieving profitability and ensuring sustainable growth:

Cost Analysis: Conduct thorough and ongoing cost analysis to gain a clear understanding of all direct and indirect expenses. This includes both variable and fixed costs, as well as hidden costs that might impact profitability. Implement advanced cost-tracking tools and software to streamline this process.

Business

Strategic Pricing: Determine appropriate pricing strategies that not only cover costs but also account for desired profit margins. Consider market research and competitor analysis to set competitive prices while ensuring profitability. Regularly revisit pricing strategies to adjust for changes in costs and market conditions.

Operational Efficiency: Streamline business operations to minimise wastage and optimise resource utilisation. Implement lean management practices and process improvements to enhance efficiency across all facets of the business.

Effective Inventory Management: For businesses with tight margins, efficient inventory management is crucial. Adopt inventory control systems to prevent overstocking or stockouts, reducing carrying costs and ensuring timely deliveries.

High-Volume Focus: In low-margin industries, prioritise volume to compensate for reduced margins. Develop strategies to increase sales volume through targeted marketing, promotions, and expanding customer reach.

Partnerships and Supplier Relations: Forge strategic partnerships with suppliers to negotiate favourable terms and prices. Collaborate with reliable partners to ensure a steady supply of quality materials at competitive rates.

Business

Advanced Financial Systems: Invest in financial management software to accurately track and analyse financial data. Leverage technology to gain insights into profitability trends, identify areas for improvement, and make informed decisions.

Long-Term Vision: While addressing immediate cash flow needs is important, maintain a focus on long-term profitability. Avoid sacrificing sustainable growth opportunities for short-term gains and consider the potential impact of decisions on the overall business trajectory.

Holistic Decision-Making: Balance short-term goals with long-term objectives by taking a comprehensive view of business decisions. Consider the impact of each decision on financial stability, customer satisfaction, and future growth prospects.

Financial Expertise: Consider seeking professional financial advice or hiring a financial expert, especially for small businesses. Their expertise can help navigate complex financial landscapes, optimise financial strategies, and ensure informed decision-making.

By adopting these strategies and tailoring them to the specific challenges faced by the business, organisations can navigate the intricacies of achieving profitability and sustainability. Balancing cost control, operational efficiency, and a long-term vision will empower businesses to overcome obstacles and establish a solid foundation for lasting success.

Business

Additional areas businesses have issues with assessing profitability:

Owner's Labour Costs:

Issue: Small business owners often invest significant time and effort into their ventures, making it difficult to assess the true cost of their labour.

Solution: Calculate the market rate for the owner's role and compare it to their hours worked. This provides insight into the potential savings if the role were outsourced or an employee was hired.

Overstocking:

Issue: Smaller businesses may accumulate excess inventory in hopes of boosting profits over the long term, potentially tying up capital and hindering cash flow.

Solution: Implement efficient inventory management systems to monitor demand trends and adjust stock levels accordingly. Focus on a just-in-time approach to reduce carrying costs while ensuring adequate supply.

Business Continuity:

Issue: Small businesses might lack proper succession planning, making it unclear whether the business can continue without the owner's involvement.

Solution: Develop a succession plan that outlines roles and responsibilities for key personnel or potential successors. Create a clear path for the business to thrive beyond the current owner's tenure.

Debt and Cost of Capital:

Issue: Owners may inject personal funds into the business without accounting for the implicit cost of capital, leading to inaccurate profitability assessment.

Solution: Assign a notional cost of capital to the owner's invested funds. This helps in evaluating whether the debt is yielding a return higher than the cost of capital, indicating genuine profitability.

Use of Owner-Owned Assets:

Issue: Owners might utilise personal assets, such as properties, without recognising the potential costs if these assets were leased externally.

Solution: Calculate the fair market value of using owner-owned assets and factor it into the cost structure. This reveals the true costs associated with asset usage and enables a more accurate assessment of profitability.

Incorporating these considerations into the profitability assessment process helps businesses uncover hidden costs and make informed decisions. By addressing these challenges head-on, businesses can better understand their true profitability, optimise operations, and ensure a more sustainable and successful future.

Effective Communication for Driving Positive Change

As an owner, you hold the power to identify crucial improvements that might elude the operational management team. However, the way you convey these insights can significantly impact their receptiveness. Striking a balance between expressing your views and being sensitive to the dynamics is essential.

It's important to recognise that many directors have a tendency to emphasise their own solutions rather than fully engaging with the team they collaborate with.

Creating an environment where constructive feedback is valued, and mistakes aren't met with demoralisation is key. Therefore, when addressing concerns, it's advisable to follow the established management process, with a focus on proposing solutions rather than fixating on shortcomings.

If you have potential solutions in mind, sharing them ahead of meetings can prove beneficial. This allows the operational management team to review and ponder these suggestions, leading to a well-prepared discussion. This approach underscores your respect for their time and encourages a collaborative atmosphere.

In some workplace settings, personal egos might overshadow the primary goal of issue resolution. By prioritising the collective objective over individual pride, a more cohesive and effective working environment can flourish.

Remember, the ultimate aim is progress, and fostering open, solution-driven dialogue ensures this objective remains at the forefront.

Building a Viable Future for the Business

Creating and formulating a forward-looking strategy involves close collaboration with the management team. It's essential to recognise that if a business doesn't reach the envisioned future state, its long-term prospects become threatened. Therefore, embarking on ambitious projects without the necessary financial capacity is essentially planning for the failure of the business.

In the past, a period of easily accessible borrowing led to a situation where many businesses could sustain significant losses over extended periods, causing distortions within the market.

Interestingly, there are numerous companies that have operated for a decade or more without managing to turn a profit. This phenomenon has been fuelled by the availability of cheap money, allowing individuals to invest and inflate the value of their shares without immediate concern for profitability.

As the cost of borrowing increases, the rationale for investing in a business with a lengthy payoff horizon diminishes.

Business

It's wiser to construct strategies based on the resources available at hand, rather than aspiring to a position that requires extensive long-term investments.

Ultimately, it's crucial to align your business ambitions with your financial capabilities. If resources are limited, it's advisable to avoid ventures that demand substantial long-term commitments and instead focus on initiatives that can generate relatively quicker returns on investment. This approach ensures that the business remains financially stable and can weather potential economic uncertainties.

When formulating a forward-looking strategy, several key principles should be considered:

Realistic Assessment: A thorough evaluation of the business's current financial health, market trends, and competitive landscape is essential. This assessment provides a realistic understanding of the resources available and the potential risks involved.

Clear Objectives: Define clear and achievable objectives that align with the business's financial capabilities. Setting overly ambitious goals without the necessary means to achieve them can lead to unsustainable practices and financial strain.

Resource Allocation: Allocate resources strategically to projects and initiatives that offer a balanced mix of short-term and long-term returns. Prioritise investments that can generate revenue and profits within a reasonable timeframe.

Business

Financial Sustainability: Strive for financial sustainability by maintaining a healthy balance between revenue generation, cost management, and investment. This approach ensures that the business can meet its financial obligations and adapt to changing market conditions.

Adaptability: Build flexibility into the strategy to adapt to unforeseen challenges and opportunities. A rigid long-term plan may become obsolete in a rapidly changing business environment.

Risk Management: Implement robust risk management practices to mitigate potential setbacks. Diversify business activities and revenue streams to reduce reliance on a single source of income.

Continuous Monitoring: Regularly monitor and evaluate the performance of strategic initiatives. If a project is not delivering the expected results within a reasonable timeframe, consider reallocating resources or adjusting the strategy accordingly.

Leverage Innovation: Explore innovative approaches to business growth that leverage technology, market trends, and customer preferences. Innovation can lead to new revenue streams and cost-saving opportunities.

Communication and Collaboration: Foster open communication and collaboration among the management team to ensure alignment and informed decision-making. Each member's expertise can contribute to a well-rounded and effective strategy.

Long-Term Viability: While focusing on short-term gains is important, also consider the long-term viability and sustainability of the business. Strive to strike a balance between immediate returns and investments that contribute to the business's enduring success.

By integrating these principles into the strategic planning process, businesses can develop a forward-looking strategy that is both ambitious and realistic, capitalising on available resources while safeguarding long-term prospects.

It is also recommended to use an A3 Strategy document.

Plan to Maintain the A3 Strategy Document

It's a common occurrence for teams to lack a unified understanding of the business and product visions, and this is typically because not everyone outside of management is ever involved with strategy discussions or even given a documented plan.

As the owner, you must remember that your team are not mind readers.

A unified understanding across teams of where the business is heading is crucial. If teams lack a unified understanding of what they're all working towards and why, priorities can be scattered, as can decision-making.

Business

This can impact business growth and even team retention, as teams will not be motivated to carry out their activities with care if they can't see the bigger picture.

With no communication system in place to ease discussion and idea sharing, the business is at risk of the silo effect occurring. The silo effect in business is when productivity and growth suffer due to a lack of communication between teams.

When teams are working toward a unified goal yet are unaware of what the other is doing to help reach the goal or of any issues the others are tackling, inconsistencies in work and inefficiencies in operations occur.

Developing a living plan that documents each team's endeavours as a business and holding regular discussion groups with teams is the easiest way to unify understandings across the company and to avoid the silo effect.

A companywide A3 Strategy Document that details your plans and purpose, and that can be reviewed on a quarterly basis by the management teams is a great tool for unifying understandings. Below is a breakdown of the components making up the document:

Goal & Purpose Statement: The Goal is a statement that motivates teams and eases business decision-making. This goal needs to be large-scale, motivating, and demanding.

Business

The Purpose statement acts as the why to your goal.

When used effectively these statements will align decisions, ensure focus across departments, and even change the direction of a business altogether, and for the better. There are a few considerations that make defining these statements a plain sailing process, or at least a little less challenging. These considerations involve asking three questions.

What is your business devoted to? Identify the elements of your business you are most passionate about. This is something that drives teams every day at work. It will interest those who share the same desires, reflect values, and retain those who agree with the importance.

Where do you want to take the market lead? Or what does your business aim to be the best at? You must question what you want the business to take the lead in and be the best at and consider what components competitors lack that you can develop. It is important to consider what products or services are not being executed well by businesses of a similar nature to yours, what could you do better?

What drives profitability within your business? What generates sustained cash flow and profitability? There is no point in being the best at something that does not prompt customers to use and buy your product or services. Analysing your product market fit will be useful at this stage.

Business

Answering these questions is an iterative process that provides insight into your economic model, what your business does best, the values of the company, and what motivates you.

Truly understanding your answers can take years. The aim of this concept is to focus on being the best at one thing, rather than being okay at multiple things.

X-Factor: A statement that describes what it is that makes your business and your team so special. It's essentially an insight into your way of doing things, your mentality, and what makes the business potentially disruptive.

Brand Promises: Define three promises your company must stick to when delivering your services, these promises help recognise any behaviour that does not align with the promises, and they can also build trust with your customers.

USP: The Unique Selling Point is what makes you different to others providing a similar service in the market. It's essentially the company party trick and north star. It's what you do differently as a business that drives customers from competitors and to your service.

Targets: These are the products, services, and processes you hope to roll out in the next 36 months.

Team Improvements: These are the key behaviours or operations the team need to work on to be the most productive they can be.

Business

Company Strengths & Weaknesses: These sections highlight what you're best at and what challenges you. You can also input your biggest opportunities and threats here.

Actions to Improve: The to-do list to tackle your weaknesses.

New Concepts & Learning: New concepts, processes, and mentality the team should work to understand.

Current Products: The products and services you have successfully developed.

Planned Products: Your initial ideas for potential products to develop in the next 60 months. These products are not fully formed business plans, just ideas, and their priority for development will depend on where the business stands later down the line.

For example, if the company sees a drop in talent retention and work capacity is at a low for teams, it will not be the best idea to start bringing in new projects.

STRATEGY DOCUMENT

Goal Statement					
Purpose (Explain the why)					
Brand Promises	Promise 1:		Promise 2:		Promise 3:
X-Factor					
Our USP					
Targets (For the next 36 months)	6 Months	12 Months	18 Months	24 Months	36 Months
Team Improvements	12 months		18 months	24 months	36 months
Company Strengths			Company Weaknesses		
Current Products			Actions to Improve		
Planned Products (60 months)			New Concepts & Learning		

STRATEGY DOCUMENT

Goal Statement	To be the leading skincare brand. Providing products that are kind to your skin.
Purpose (Explain the why)	We work to provide skincare that is kind to our planet and kind to mankind.

Brand Promises

Promise 1: To only use natural ingredients that are kind to your skin.	Promise 2: To produce and deliver our products in a way that is kind to our plant.	Promise 3: To be accessible and affordable worldwide.

X-Factor	Every team member understands the importance of cross-functionality and has completed ThoseWhoCode course.
Our USP	From kind ingredients and kind prices to kind packaging and kind delivery. Every aspect of our product, customer service, and business model is kind to the planet and those living on it.

Targets (For the next 36 months)

6 Months	12 Months	18 Months	24 Months	36 Months
Launch the ToBeKind Book. Introduce the ToBeKind podcast series & subscription. Continue development of eyecare products.	Continue working on subscription and podcast material. Launch eyecare range. Develop Affiliate Marketing channels using the blog.	Development of ToBeKind: Planet Edition book. Review Affiliate Marketing channels. Introduce live podcast shows.	Launch of ToBeKind: Planet Edition book. Develop Revitalising Oil.	Launch Revitalising Oil.

Team Improvements

12 months	18 months	24 months	36 months
Product team to have fully completed the Beauty Decoded course. Remote Digital Marketing apprenticeships introduced to develop the Marketing team.	Kind lifestyle scheme implemented in the UK.	Scrum process to be followed by all members.	Week-long team building retreat numbers confirmed.

Company Strengths

We are a small company with a strong understanding of kind skincare and are eager to learn.

We recognise the pros of distributed working and hiring a team based on skills, not location.

We understand the importance of employee well-being and we wish to host an inclusive workplace.

Company Weaknesses

The market is changing on a regular basis while we are still learning.

There are only 12 staff members.

It takes a while to bring products to market.

Current Products	ToBeKind soap, lotion, and hair mask. ToBeKind YouTube series.
Actions to Improve	More staff on board for R&D. Agile product development fully implemented.
New Concepts & Learning	Understand the importance of accountability and responsibility in work. Understand how to improve productivity - Automation for example.
Planned Products (60 months)	Books, Podcast Series, Eyecare, Subscription, Live show, Oil.

Business

It is important to conduct reviews with stakeholders within your business to validate and confirm the commitment to implementing this strategy.

For optimal efficiency, distribute the strategy document on a Friday, preferably towards the end of the workday. This schedule provides stakeholders with the entire weekend to thoroughly review the document and gain a clear understanding of the outlined requirements.

An A3 Meeting Plan is another great tool for unifying understandings within the business teams and other stakeholders. This document details the tasks/projects/issues to be tackled, the date of project kick-off, elements or dependencies required to help complete the project, the names of the people tackling the project, any potential risks, and the completion date.

This document is to be used, updated, and shared monthly within the management and junior teams, as it helps unify an understanding of what teams should be focusing on. Therefore, no priority work should fall behind.

On the following page is a template and an example of the document in progress.

Date:

Topics of discussion/issues to be resolved:	Ready to start:	Elements that are required to complete:	Person responsible:	Issues/dependencies:	Deadline:

Topics of discussion/issues to be resolved:	Ready to start:	Elements that are required to complete:	Person responsible:	Issues:	Deadline:
Is the development of the www.examplewebsite.com landing page, about page, booking page, and booking/contact forms completed?	3/11	Zoho to be set up. Stripe fixed and activated for card payments. Yoastseo	Mark Morgan	Customers receiving failed payment message but then it goes through. Customers are making multiple purchases	
Please add the following content to www.examplewebsite.com: • Ex1 • Ex2 • Ex3	4/11	Use jasper copywriter	Megan		
www.examplewebsite.com FAQ videos developed?	5/11	Vimeo and Loom set up	Kate		
www.examplewebsite.com Zoho mapping to contact and booking forms.	4/11	Upgrade Zoho. Gravity forms need adjusting to communicate with Zoho for mapping	Morgan	Fields not fully mapping	
Progress to be made on subscription service. A content plan formed. Monetisation ideas.	4/11	Research	Mark		
Google ads how many customers for Sept 2022, Oct 2022? CAC costs – New Customers?	9/11		Kate		
Review of new ads, are we ready to go?	9/11	Competitor research	Kate	Ad strength poor	

Teams & Decision-Making

One of the best ways you can support the development of your business is to allow your management teams to make their own decisions from the start. This autonomy not only encourages your team to reflect and revise their decision-making processes (which is important for skill growth) but prevents you as management from micro-managing every move made in the business.

With coaching and guidance from seniors, your team must learn to make their own decisions within the business as soon as they become part of the company. By allowing them to make their own decisions, you are supporting the development of trust in their relationship with you and are pushing a sense of responsibility and accountability.

With a sense of responsibility and the confidence to make their own decisions, your team will be able to keep their head whenever you are not available to answer questions or to decide for them. Through trial and error, they will become better decision-makers.

It is important to note, that if you're allowing your team to make their own decisions you must be able to forgive and forget when a mistake occurs with a decision made. Mistakes are part of the learning process, and your team will not be able to confidently make decisions if they feel they will be scorned if they get it wrong.

Coaching Decisions

The SAARA model for decision-making is a process you should familiarise your teams with. This process offers tips that will help your team make educated decisions. Ask them to use the following process:

Step Back from the situation. If you are on the phone and are asked to decide or have an opinion on something, say that you will call them back in 15 minutes once you have fully processed the information. This gives you the breathing space to think and it stops you from making an immediate decision out of pressure.

Assess the options available. When you first start the reflection and review process, write down the options available and the risks aligned with all options. This will help rule out any no-goes. It is also a clever idea to determine the weight of the decision. For example, if a decision impacts the future of the business, finances, a client, or you simply can't go back on it once it's made, it's a good idea to inform the person who will be most affected by the decision and get them involved with the process.

Ask For Help, if the decision to be made is an immediate concern or it seems like every option is a poor move, run the situation by a coach, mentor, teammate, or manager. By discussing the situation, you become open to new interpretations and perspectives, and it helps lift the weight of dealing with the situation on your own.

Review the options that are available. At this stage, a review is more than just reflecting on the risks. Take time to ask questions regarding the direction of the business and how each option available supports or impacts the direction.

Action Your Decision, now it's time to put your decision into action, if you get it wrong this time you will learn from the experience and improve your decision-making process for the next.

It's important to remember that if you get the decision wrong, assess whether you could have made the correct decision with the information available at the time, not the information you have today.

We improve our decision-making process by increasing the number of decisions we make. If a change in the situation occurs, then review your decision using the same process.

Below is a detailed dive into decision-making considerations:

Are you the right person to make the decision? Review the impact on the business and how long it could last. If the impact is minimal, you may be the right person to address the situation. On the other hand, if the impact is substantial and potentially involves a long-term influence or a considerable sum of money coming out, it will be wise to raise the situation with management/directors.

Business

When situations like this arise, it's important (even if you don't make the decision in the end) to assess the decision that you would have made and be comfortable in defending your decision.

Is the decision low-impact or high-impact? Whether you are confused by the number of options available to you or conflicted by the consequences of each, analysing the level of the decision in terms of high-impact or low-impact is a process that can help you clearly compare whether you're the right person to determine the solution.

A low-impact decision is one that has minimal influence on the business, while a high-impact decision is one that can significantly alter the outcome and have a lasting influence.

The distinction between the two can be based on factors such as the level of risk involved, the resources required, the limitations of the business, the potential benefits, and the long-term impact of the decision's influence.

Signing a new lease, mergers, investing, and restructuring operations are high-impact decisions.

Following a model that reviews the level of risk and impact, as a business, can prevent management and teams from wasting time on making decisions that are not theirs to make.

Business

Decision-Making Risk Management Matrix

As a business owner, you can visualise and determine the level of risk associated with a decision to be made before taking the next steps, using a Decision-Making Risk Management Matrix. This matrix works by ensuring you consider the factors that increase risks, the total value of the transaction, and the potential value of the transaction to understand the possible threats and opportunities regarding a decision to be made.

From here you can then determine the level of risk associated with the decision ranging from low to high, and then plan the next steps.

On the following pages is an example of the matrix in process and a template to use for your own decision-making.

Decision Making Risk Management Matrix:

This matrix ensures you can visualise & determine the level of risk associated with a decision before taking the next steps.

Once you have considered and filled out the *Decision to be made, Factors that increase risks, Total Value of Transaction, and Potential Value of Transaction* sections of the canvas and understand the potential threats and opportunities, you can TICK the level of risk associated with the decision ranging from low to high, and then plan the next steps as a business.

Decision to be made:	Factors that increase risks:	Methods of reducing risk:	Total Value of Transaction:	Potential Value of Transaction:	Level 1 Low	Level 2	Level 3	Level 4	Level 5 High
5-year lease: £40,000 with no break clause. Full Repairing and Insuring Lease.	Building requiring full repair. Landlord requires the building to be returned to high standard. Director Guaranteed increasing the chances of problems occurring.	Requiring the building being up to standard before accepting the lease. Refusing Director Guaranteed in place. Use of deposit instead.	£200,000 Possible repair cost at end of lease.	Up to £250,000				✓	
Publishing books	Brand Damage. Litigation due to trademark infringement. Use of images without licences. Hard to assess total and potential value of transaction until we recognise demand. Legal fees for breaching trademark.	Use separate limited company to reduce risk of brand damage. Check for use of trademarks. Use one of the royalty free picture websites. Keep records of pictures and use.	Hard to assess total value of transaction until we recognise demand. Hard to assess due to potential trademark breach costs.	Hard to assess potential value of transaction until we recognise demand. Hard to assess due to potential trademark breach costs.		✓			

Decision Making Risk Management Matrix:

This matrix ensures you can visualise & determine the level of risk associated with a decision before taking the next steps.

Once you have considered and filled out the *Decision to be made, Factors that increase risks, Total Value of Transaction, and Potential Value of Transaction* sections of the canvas and understand the potential threats and opportunities, you can **TICK** the **level of risk** associated with the decision ranging from low to high, and then plan the next steps as a business.

Decision to be made:	Factors that increase risks:	Methods of reducing risk:	Total Value of Transaction:	Potential Value of Transaction:	Level 1 Low	Level 2	Level 3	Level 4	Level 5 High

Business

Dealing With Recessions & Emergency Situations

As a business owner, having the skills necessary to navigate through challenging periods such as recessions or emergency situations is essential.

A recession is an economic downturn, caused by factors such as reduced consumer spending, decreased business investment, rising unemployment rates, and contraction in the overall economy. During a recession, businesses often face decreased demand for their products or services, tightening credit conditions, and increased competition for limited resources.

In addition to recessions, businesses can also encounter emergency situations, such as supply chain disruptions, a public health crisis, or unexpected market shifts. These emergency situations can cause disruptions to operations, impact customer demand, and create financial constraints.

Both recessions and emergency situations can have significant implications for businesses. It is crucial for business owners to be prepared and equipped to navigate these challenges effectively.

This includes having the skills to:

Implement sound financial management practices: Regular accounts management allows business owners to closely monitor their cash flow, including incoming revenues and outgoing expenses.

Business

During a recession, cash flow becomes even more critical as businesses may experience reduced sales or delayed payments.

By keeping a close eye on cash flow and implementing strategies to optimise it, such as controlling costs, negotiating better payment terms with suppliers, or managing inventory efficiently, business owners can ensure they have sufficient liquidity to weather the downturn.

Regular accounts management enables business owners to spot potential financial warning signs early on. By reviewing financial statements, profit and loss reports, balance sheets, and cash flow statements on a monthly basis, owners can identify any negative trends or anomalies that may indicate financial distress. This early detection allows them to take proactive measures to address the issues promptly, such as implementing cost-cutting measures, adjusting pricing strategies, or seeking additional funding if needed.

Accurate and up-to-date financial information obtained through monthly accounts management provides business owners with a solid foundation for strategic decision-making during a recession. It helps them evaluate the business's financial health, assess the performance of various product lines or business segments, and identify areas that require improvement.

Business

This information allows owners to make informed decisions about resource allocation, investment priorities, and potential cost-saving measures to sustain the business during challenging times.

By maintaining disciplined financial management practices before, during, and after a recession, business owners position themselves for recovery and future growth. When economic conditions start to improve, businesses that have managed their finances carefully are better equipped to capitalise on emerging opportunities, invest in strategic initiatives, and quickly ramp up operations.

They can leverage their financial stability to gain a competitive edge and accelerate growth as the economy rebounds.

Identify when an emergency situation may occur and act quickly: Identifying when an emergency situation or recession may occur can be challenging, as there is often a gap between when discussions about a potential downturn begin and when it actually materialises. However, there are some indicators that business owners can monitor to assess the likelihood of an impending recession or emergency situation.

Paying attention to key economic indicators can provide insights into the overall health of the economy. These indicators include GDP growth rates, employment figures, consumer spending, business investment, and manufacturing activity.

Business

Monitoring these indicators can help business owners identify any signs of a potential economic downturn.

Changes in interest rates can provide indications of economic conditions. Banks often adjust interest rates to manage inflation and stimulate or cool down the economy. A significant increase in interest rates may indicate a bank's effort to combat inflation or curb excessive borrowing, which can be a precursor to an economic slowdown or recession.

The housing market is often closely tied to economic conditions. Changes in house prices can provide clues about the state of the economy. A sudden decline in house prices or a slowdown in housing transactions may indicate a softening economy, reduced consumer confidence, and a potential downturn.

Monitoring consumer sentiment surveys and consumer spending patterns can provide insights into the overall confidence and financial well-being of individuals. During times of economic uncertainty or leading up to a recession, consumer sentiment tends to become more cautious, and spending may decrease as individuals prepare for potential financial challenges. People may cancel memberships and subscription services.

Assessing business sentiment and investment intentions can also offer clues about the direction of the economy.

Business

If businesses show signs of reduced confidence, scale back expansion plans, or decrease capital investments, it could indicate a more cautious outlook and potential economic stress.

By keeping a vigilant eye on these indicators and staying informed about market trends and economic developments, business owners can be better prepared to navigate potential emergency situations or economic downturns. This includes implementing risk management strategies, ensuring financial stability, and being proactive in adjusting business plans and operations to adapt to changing market conditions.

Focus on what your business needs to survive: Navigating a recession or emergency requires business owners to prioritise their business's survival and make strategic decisions to weather the storm effectively.

During a recession, it is vital for business owners to resist the temptation of comparing themselves to others and focusing too much on external factors. Getting caught up in the effects on other businesses can divert attention from what truly matters - identifying and implementing strategies to protect and sustain your own business.

Each business is unique, and the focus should be on tailored approaches and solutions that best suit your specific circumstances.

Moreover, business owners must be aware that not all information about other businesses is entirely truthful.

Business

Some may attribute their struggles solely to external factors, such as the recession or an emergency situation, without acknowledging pre-existing challenges. It is crucial to rely on accurate data, conduct a thorough analysis, and base decisions on understanding one's own business strengths, weaknesses, and market dynamics.

One of the most challenging aspects of navigating a recession is maintaining profits and taking swift action when making changes to teams or operations.

Business owners must continually assess the performance of their business units, identify inefficiencies, and make difficult decisions to optimise operations, such as turning to automation. This may involve restructuring, cost reduction measures, or strategic shifts to capitalise on emerging opportunities.

Additionally, calling the end of a recession in the real business world can be challenging. While government agencies may declare the official end of a recession based on specific economic indicators, the impact on individual businesses may lag behind. Business owners must stay vigilant, monitor market trends, and make informed judgments based on their business's performance, customer demand, and overall economic conditions.

Focusing on what your business needs to survive during a recession or emergency situation is a critical skill for business owners.

Business

It involves staying alert to market conditions, avoiding distractions from others' experiences, relying on accurate information, and taking decisive action to maintain profitability and adapt operations as necessary. By honing this skill, business owners can enhance their resilience and position their businesses for long-term success, even in challenging times.

During a recession or emergency situation, focusing on customer retention becomes paramount. Business owners should prioritise maintaining strong relationships with existing customers, providing excellent customer service, and adapting their products or services to meet changing customer needs and preferences. This customer-centric approach can help businesses weather the storm by fostering loyalty and sustaining revenue streams.

Clear and transparent communication with employees, stakeholders, and customers is crucial during challenging times. Business owners should proactively communicate updates, changes in operations, and strategies to mitigate the impact of the recession or emergency situation. Transparent communication helps build trust, maintain morale, and manage expectations, fostering a sense of unity and collective effort to overcome difficulties.

In the face of a recession or emergency, businesses need to be agile and open to innovation.

Business

Business owners should encourage a culture of adaptability, encourage creative problem-solving, and explore new opportunities or business models that align with changing market dynamics.

Being flexible and open to change can position businesses to seize emerging opportunities and stay ahead of the curve.

Going Into a Recession

There are a number of factors to focus on when going into a recession as a business owner, by considering and addressing each of these following points, you can proactively prepare for a recession, minimise risks, and make informed decisions to navigate through challenging times successfully:

Parachute for business failure: First of all, it is crucial for you yourself to have a contingency plan in case your business faces financial difficulties or goes under. You must assess whether you have measures in place to protect yourself and ensure your financial well-being. This may include personal savings and alternative income sources.

It is equally as important to review whether you have previously signed any director guarantees and understand your personal liability. If you have signed director guarantees and your business is going under, you can take the following steps to explore potential options for resolving financial difficulties:

Business

- Seek legal advice: Consult with a qualified attorney or solicitor experienced in corporate law or insolvency. They can provide guidance on your legal rights, potential liabilities, and options available to you in the given situation.

- Open communication with creditors: Initiate open and honest communication with your creditors. Inform them about the financial challenges your business is facing and discuss possible solutions. Some creditors may be willing to negotiate payment terms or come to a settlement arrangement.

- Negotiate with creditors: Engage in negotiations with your creditors to reach agreements on debt repayment terms or settlements that are manageable for both parties. Exploring options like debt forgiveness or debt-to-equity conversions may also be beneficial.

- Explore restructuring options: Consider restructuring options for your business, such as debt restructuring, refinancing, or seeking assistance from insolvency practitioners. These professionals can provide advice on potential restructuring or insolvency procedures that may help alleviate the financial burden on your business and limit personal liability.

- Consider insolvency procedures: If the financial situation is irreparable, you may need to consider formal insolvency procedures such as voluntary liquidation or administration. Consult with insolvency professionals who can guide you through the process and help manage the affairs of the business in a controlled manner.

- Protect personal assets: Take steps to protect your personal assets to the extent possible within the legal framework. Consult with your legal advisor to understand how best to safeguard your personal finances and assets from being implicated in the business's financial troubles.

- Document all decisions and actions: Maintain thorough documentation of all decisions, communications, and actions taken during this process. This will help demonstrate that you have acted responsibly and in accordance with legal obligations.

Cash burn and bill coverage: Evaluate your current cash burn rate, which refers to the rate at which your business is consuming cash to cover expenses. Determine if you have sufficient funds to sustain your operations during a recession. Assess your ability to cover essential bills, such as rent, utilities, and payroll, and consider potential cost-cutting measures to extend your cash runway.

Business

Emergency cash reserves: Calculate how long you can sustain your business using your emergency cash reserves. Determine the duration that your reserves can cover your expenses without any incoming revenue. This will give you a clearer understanding of how much time you have to make necessary adjustments, secure additional funding, or explore alternative business strategies.

Balancing cash reserves: While having a significant amount of cash reserves can provide a safety net during a recession, it is important to be cautious. Relying solely on cash reserves may delay addressing underlying issues or making hard decisions that are necessary for the long-term survival of your business. Use cash reserves wisely and ensure that you are actively addressing the root causes of financial challenges to sustain your business in the long run.

High-risk liabilities: Identify any high-risk liabilities that may pose a threat to your business's financial stability during a recession. These may include leases with personal guarantees, debts secured under your own name, or debts owed to the government. Evaluate the potential impact of these liabilities and consider strategies to manage or reduce them, such as renegotiating terms, seeking financial assistance, or exploring alternative arrangements.

Business

Monitoring profitability: Regularly monitor your business's profitability on a monthly basis. Assess key financial indicators, such as revenue, expenses, profit margins, and cash flow, to gain insights into your business's financial health. This monitoring enables you to identify any negative trends or areas that require improvement promptly, allowing you to take corrective actions and make necessary adjustments to enhance profitability.

Reducing liability and improving profitability: During a recession, cash preservation becomes crucial. If cash is available, consider strategies to reduce your liability and improve profitability. For example, you may negotiate discounts with suppliers to purchase stock at lower costs, thus enhancing profitability. Evaluate your expenses critically and look for opportunities to reduce costs without compromising the quality of your products or services.

Diversifying client base: Assess whether your business relies heavily on a single client or a few key clients who account for a significant portion of your turnover. During a recession, the risk of client liquidation or administration increases. To mitigate this risk, aim to diversify your client base by attracting new customers and expanding your reach.

This will help reduce the impact of losing a single client and enhance the stability of your business during challenging times.

Currency risk management: If your business operates internationally or deals with foreign currencies, consider the potential impact of currency fluctuations on your financial stability. Evaluate the options for protecting against currency risk, such as entering into forward contracts or using financial instruments that protect against adverse exchange rate movements. Implementing appropriate currency risk management strategies can help protect your business from financial volatility and uncertainty.

Reducing Costs

In an emergency situation, it is important for businesses to act quickly. This means reducing unnecessary costs, such as expensive office space and software that is no longer required. Businesses should also automate tasks that can be automated, such as email and CRM. This can help to increase productivity and save money.

There are various types of automation.

Semi-automated processes are those that still require some input from human team members, but they reduce the amount of work that those team members need to do.

For example, a coffee shop might introduce automatic coffee machines that require a team member to load the beans and milk, but the machines then grind the beans, brew the coffee, and dispense it into cups.

Business

The team member still needs to be present to load the machines and take payment, but they don't need to do any of the actual brewing or dispensing.

Here are some other examples of semi-automated processes:

- Self-checkout registers at grocery stores.
- Automated customer service chatbots.
- Automated lead generation software.
- Automated marketing campaigns.

Semi-automated processes offer a number of benefits for businesses, including:

- Increased efficiency: Semi-automated processes can help businesses to reduce the amount of time and labour required to complete tasks. This can lead to increased productivity and profitability.

- Reduced costs: Semi-automated processes can help businesses to reduce costs in a number of ways, such as by reducing the need for human labour and by eliminating the need for manual data entry.

- Improved accuracy: Semi-automated processes can help businesses to improve accuracy by reducing the risk of human error.

- Increased customer satisfaction: Semi-automated processes can help businesses to improve customer satisfaction by providing faster and more convenient service.

Fully automated processes are those that require no input from human team members. They are the most complex and difficult to implement, but they can offer the greatest benefits for businesses.

For example, a fully automated coffee shop would have robots that grind the beans, brew the coffee, dispense it into cups, and take payment.

Here are some other examples of fully automated processes:

- Automated assembly lines in manufacturing plants.
- Automated warehouses and distribution centres.
- Automated customer service call centres.
- Automated trading systems.

Fully automated processes offer a number of benefits for businesses, including:

- Extreme efficiency: Fully automated processes can be extremely efficient, as they can operate 24/7 without the need for human intervention.

- Reduced costs: Fully automated processes can help businesses to reduce costs by eliminating the need for human labour.

- Increased accuracy: Fully automated processes can help businesses to improve accuracy by eliminating the risk of human error.

- Increased scalability: Fully automated processes can be easily scaled up or down to meet the needs of a business.

However, fully automated processes also have some challenges, including:

- High upfront costs: The implementation of fully automated processes can be expensive.

- Complexity: Fully automated processes can be complex to design, implement, and maintain.

- Risk of downtime: If a fully automated process breaks down, it can cause significant disruption to a business.

If you are facing a recession, you may want to consider implementing a semi-automated process as a way to reduce costs and improve efficiency.

This can help you to weather the storm and emerge from the recession stronger than ever before.

For example, instead of handling support operations over the phone, would it be better to tackle issues over email or a support ticket feature?

This means teams can focus on resolving multiple cases simultaneously rather than being tied up on the phone with one customer at a time. Additionally, using automated responses or chatbots for common queries can further reduce the workload on your support teams.

There are some steps that you should take as a business if you're considering turning to automation:

- Assess your needs: The first step is to assess your needs and identify the areas in your business that could benefit from automation, such as repetitive tasks. This will help you to determine the type of automation that is right for you.

- Do your research: Once you have identified the areas that you want to automate, it is important to do your research and understand the different automation technologies available. This will help you to choose the right technology for your needs and budget.

- Create a business case: Before you invest in automation, it is important to create a business case that outlines the benefits of automation and the costs associated with it. This will help you to justify the investment and make sure that it is a good fit for your business.

- Get buy-in from your team: It is important to get buy-in from your team before you implement automation. This will help to ensure that everyone is on board with the changes and that the automation is successful.

- Plan for the transition: Once you have made the decision to automate, it is important to plan for the transition. This includes training your team on the new technology and making sure that your systems are compatible with the new automation.

- Monitor and adjust: Once automation is in place, it is important to monitor its performance and make adjustments as needed. This will help you to ensure that the automation is meeting your needs and that it is still a good fit for your business.

Here are some additional tips for businesses considering automation:

- Start small: If you are new to automation, it is a good idea to start small and automate one or two processes at a time. This will help you to learn about the process and make sure that it is a good fit for your business.

- Focus on high-volume, repetitive tasks: Automation is most effective when it is used to automate high-volume, repetitive tasks. This is because automation can quickly and efficiently complete these tasks, which can save you time and money.

- Consider your budget: When choosing automation technology, it is important to consider your budget. There are a variety of automation technologies available at different price points. It is important to choose the technology that is right for your needs and budget.

- Make sure your systems are compatible: Before you implement automation, it is important to make sure that your systems are compatible with the new technology. This will help to avoid any problems during the transition.

- Get help from experts: If you are not sure how to implement automation, it is a good idea to get help from experts. There are a number of companies that specialise in helping businesses automate their processes, such as Zoho One.

Here are some other ways to reduce business costs to prepare for a recession or emergency situation:

Business

- Negotiate better prices with suppliers: If you are a large business, you may be able to negotiate better prices with your suppliers. This can save you a significant amount of money on your purchases.

- Review your insurance policies: It is important to review your insurance policies regularly to make sure that you are getting the best possible coverage for your business. You may be able to save money by switching to a different insurance company or by changing your coverage.

- Cut back on marketing and advertising: If you are not generating enough sales, it may be a good idea to cut back on your marketing and advertising expenses. This can save you a lot of money in the short term.

- Restructure your business: If your business is not profitable, you may need to restructure your business. This could involve laying off employees, closing unprofitable branches, or changing your product or service offerings.

- Focus on your core competencies: During a recession, it is important to focus on your core competencies. This means focusing on the things that you do best and that you can do more efficiently than your competitors.

- Be flexible: During a recession, it is important to be flexible and adaptable. This means being willing to change your business model or your operations if necessary.

- Research and take advantage of government programs: There are a number of government programs available to help businesses during a recession, such as business rates relief and small business grants. These programs can provide you with financial assistance, tax breaks, and other resources.

By taking these steps, you can reduce your business costs and prepare for a recession or emergency situation.

The Use of Technology to Reduce Inflation

Reducing inflation is a significant economic challenge, and a powerful solution lies in leveraging technology to enhance productivity. By using advanced technology, businesses and industries can work smarter, produce more, and use resources efficiently. This method has the potential to create a positive impact on overall productivity and help control rising prices.

Here's how it works: Integrating technology into various sectors, such as manufacturing and services, leads to automation and improved accuracy.

Tools like artificial intelligence and data-driven insights enable businesses to do more with less effort. This heightened efficiency not only leads to increased production but also helps prevent prices from surging due to inefficiency.

Furthermore, the benefits aren't confined to individual sectors. As industries adopt technology and become more productive, it fuels competition and innovation. This ripple effect can trigger broader economic improvements that ultimately counteract inflationary pressures.

While harnessing technology to enhance productivity offers a promising avenue for reducing inflation, it's crucial to remember that technology has its limitations and can also impact the customer experience.

Take, for example, the simple act of getting a cup of coffee. If a customer enters a café seeking not just a beverage but also a friendly conversation or a cozy atmosphere, the purely transactional nature of automated systems might fall short of meeting their expectations. Incorporating advanced technology, such as self-service kiosks or mobile ordering, can expedite the coffee-ordering process, reduce labour costs, and contribute to overall productivity.

However, there's a delicate balance to strike.

For customers seeking a personal touch or a brief moment of connection, the absence of human interaction might leave them feeling unsatisfied or disconnected from the experience.

Moreover, technology may inadvertently create a divide between those who embrace and have access to it, and those who do not. The digital divide could lead to exclusion or a sense of alienation among certain customer segments, intensifying the challenge of ensuring a positive and inclusive customer experience.

To navigate these challenges, businesses must carefully consider the role of technology in their customer interactions. While automation and efficiency are crucial, maintaining a human element – particularly for services where personal interaction is valued – remains essential. Incorporating technology in a way that complements and enhances the customer experience rather than replaces it can strike a harmonious balance between productivity and customer satisfaction.

In summary, using technology to enhance productivity offers a compelling strategy for tackling inflation. By embracing innovation, streamlining processes, and fostering adaptability, businesses can set a course for economic stability. As the digital landscape continues to evolve, the potential to reduce inflation through technology remains a promising avenue, guiding economies towards a more balanced and prosperous future.

While automation and cost reduction are vital, they must be harmonised with the desire for personal connection and a positive customer experience. By thoughtfully navigating these challenges, businesses can capitalise on the benefits of technology while ensuring that customers continue to enjoy meaningful interactions and satisfaction.

Banking Protection

As a business owner, you need to understand the significance of safeguarding your business through proper banking protection measures. It is important to consider the potential consequences that could arise if the financial institution where your business holds its funds were to face insolvency.

Are you equipped to endure a prolonged period without access to your funds? Or would your business suffer severe repercussions as a result?

While banks are generally considered secure and reliable, unforeseen circumstances such as economic downturns, financial crisis, or mismanagement can lead to their downfall. In such situations, account holders may encounter difficulties in accessing their funds promptly, potentially causing substantial disruptions to their businesses.

It is important to note that in the United Kingdom, only a certain amount of your deposits in a bank are guaranteed by the government if the bank goes into administration.

Business

This guarantee is provided by the Financial Services Compensation Scheme (FSCS), which protects deposits up to £85,000 per person, per banking institution. If your business holds more funds than the guaranteed amount, there is a risk of losing a significant portion of your deposits in the event of a bank failure. It is crucial to consider this limitation when evaluating the level of protection offered by your bank.

The inability to make payroll due to banking disruptions can create significant stress and disruptions to your business operations. Your employees depend on their salaries to meet financial commitments, and any delay or inability to pay them on time can lead to demotivation, decreased productivity, and potential legal implications.

Moreover, the failure to meet payroll obligations can damage your business's reputation and employee morale, making it challenging to retain talent and maintain a positive work environment. It is essential to have contingency plans in place, such as maintaining cash reserves or establishing alternative banking relationships, to ensure that your business can meet payroll obligations even in the face of banking disruptions.

To mitigate the potential negative consequences, it is recommended to diversify your banking relationships and allocate funds across multiple trusted financial institutions.

This strategy helps distribute the risk and ensures that even if one bank faces difficulties, your business will still have access to other funds. By diversifying, you reduce the likelihood of losing access to all your resources and can maintain essential operations during uncertain times.

Opting for a bank with a long-standing history and a reputation for stability can potentially reduce the risk of encountering banking problems. Banks that have demonstrated successful operations over a considerable period often exhibit robust financial management practices and a solid industry reputation.

In the event of financial difficulties, these banks may be more likely to receive support from the government or regulatory authorities. While government intervention is not guaranteed, regulators typically prioritise stabilising large, systemically important institutions to prevent widespread economic repercussions.

However, it is important to note that past stability does not guarantee future performance, and it is still crucial to stay informed about the financial health and stability of your chosen bank.

Regularly monitoring the news, financial reports, and market conditions can help you identify any warning signs or concerns related to the institutions holding your business's funds.

This proactive approach enables you to make informed decisions and take timely action if necessary, such as transferring funds or seeking alternative banking arrangements to safeguard your business's financial well-being.

Change in the Cost of Capital

It is essential to acknowledge that the cost of capital is experiencing fluctuations. Presently, the cost of capital remains relatively high, averaging around 6%. This holds considerable importance for making investment decisions in your business, as it directly impacts the appeal of various opportunities.

For example, ventures that demand significant capital, such as farming, exemplify the high-risk nature and limited returns associated with them.

Conducting a basic analysis, it becomes evident that these ventures require investments of one million or more, with no guarantee of returns due to the inherent risks arising from unpredictable crop yields and market prices.

As of August 2023, UK banks offer a risk-free rate of 5.5% through fixed bond investments.

When evaluating potential investments for your business, it is essential to determine the minimum rate of return you require to justify the risk involved.

Business

Assessing the risk associated with achieving that desired rate of return becomes a critical consideration in the investment decision-making process.

Below are basic examples of the types of return (not investment advice):

*This table is excluding taxes.

Type of Investment	Investment requirements	Cash return or other returns	Cash return after costs	Rate of return % per year	Total value of return over the investment period	Potential upsides
Letting an office building	£300,000	£30,000 per year	£23,000	7.67%	5-year investment period is £115,000	Increase in property value
Productivity software	£30,000	£27000 per year reduction in staffing costs	£27000	90%	5-year investment period is £135,000	Resale to other providers

Here are the formulas for calculating the rate of return % per year and the total value of return over the investment period:

Rate of Return % per Year:

Rate of Return % = (Cash Return after Costs / Investment Requirements) * 100

Total Value of Return over the Investment Period:

Total Return = Cash Return after Costs * Number of Years

Business

"Cash Return after Costs" is the amount of money you receive after deducting any associated costs.

"Investment Requirements" is the initial amount you invested.

"Number of Years" is the duration of the investment period.

To make wise decisions about investments, it's important to really understand how it all works.

Think of it like solving a puzzle with moving pieces. The investment world can be unpredictable because the prices of stocks and assets can suddenly go up or down. This uncertainty comes from market volatility.

Changes in the economy, which affect interest rates and global trade, add another layer of complexity, and then there are unexpected events like trade disputes or political changes that can also affect how investments perform.

All these factors can influence how much money you might make or lose from an investment. It's important to align your investment choices with your financial goals, risk tolerance, and time horizon. Staying informed and continually learning about the factors influencing the market can help you make more informed and strategic investment decisions.

Business

Pivoting the Business and Methods Used

A business may need to pivot for various reasons, such as changes in market conditions, shifts in customer preferences, disruptive technologies, or emerging competition. Pivoting quickly is of utmost importance due to the dynamic nature of business environments. Delaying necessary changes can lead to missed opportunities, loss of competitive advantage, or even business failure.

Being agile and responsive to market shifts allows businesses to adapt, innovate, and seize new opportunities in a timely manner, ensuring long-term sustainability and growth.

Pivoting a business and implementing new methods can be a challenging endeavour. The speed at which this is done is crucial due to the limited bandwidth within teams to accommodate these changes. People within the organisation prefer to see progress being made, so if you alter the team's objective or their role within it, they will give you a certain amount of time to make the necessary adjustments. However, this time frame is limited.

To effectively pivot a business, a simple method can be employed:

Research: Thoroughly investigate and evaluate the need for a change in objective. Explore all available options before deciding to pivot from the current idea.

Business

It's important to understand the rationale behind the decision and the potential impact it may have on the business.

Planning: Strike a balance between planning and taking action. While planning is essential, too much focus on the plan itself can hinder recognising the urgent need for change. Ensure that the planning phase is productive and leads to actionable steps.

Changing the strategic plan: Modify the strategic plan for the team, aligning it with the new objective or direction. Clearly communicate the changes and provide guidance on how the team's efforts should be redirected. It is crucial to get buy-in from the team and ensure they understand the reasons behind the pivot.

Agreeing on the plan: Reach a consensus within the team regarding the plan moving forward. This agreement should be made swiftly to maintain momentum and avoid unnecessary delays. Encourage active participation and engagement from team members to foster a sense of ownership and commitment to the new direction.

Early wins and trust-building: Incorporate small wins into the plan early on. Achieving these milestones reinforces the belief that the team is on the right track and builds trust within the leadership. Celebrate successes and acknowledge the efforts of the team to maintain motivation and engagement.

Completing the minimum viable product (MVP): Focus on rapidly completing the plan and reaching the minimum viable product stage as soon as possible. This allows for comprehensive testing and validation of the new idea or approach. Gathering feedback and data during this stage is vital in determining the feasibility and potential success of the pivot.

Case Study: A Pivot Towards Hygiene Innovation

In 2017, a company was established to address the inconvenience of depleting phone batteries while on the move. The company's vision involved creating a network of smart charging stations in various public venues, such as cafes, bars, and airports. These stations offered users the convenience of borrowing portable chargers for their devices, which could be returned to any station within the network.

However, by early 2020, the emergence of the COVID-19 pandemic posed unforeseen challenges. Public health concerns prompted a significant decrease in the demand for communal facilities like phone charging stations. Recognising the potential threats to their business model, the company acknowledged the need for adaptation to ensure survival.

In response, the company's leadership embarked on extensive market research to identify new opportunities for growth and sustainability.

Business

Their research highlighted the growing importance of touchless solutions due to the increased emphasis on hand sanitisation for public safety. This insight led to the exploration of a new direction for the company's offerings.

Drawing inspiration from their research, the company conceptualised a smart hand sanitisation solution that could utilise their existing network of charging stations. The new solution aimed to provide touch-free hand sanitisation options in public spaces. The company undertook the task of retrofitting their charging stations with hand sanitisation dispensers, incorporating contactless sensors and IoT technology to ensure a completely touchless experience. The chosen hand sanitisers were also chosen for their eco-friendly and refillable attributes, aligning with the company's commitment to sustainability.

This innovative solution was introduced to the market during the peak of the pandemic in mid-2020. The company strategically partnered with local authorities, businesses, and public venues to install the new dispensers in high-traffic areas. To ensure ongoing maintenance and refills, the company offered a subscription-based model for businesses.

The pivot to the new hygiene-focused solution proved to be transformative for the company. This strategic shift not only ensured the company's survival during the pandemic but also enabled it to thrive in the new market landscape.

The public embraced the touchless and sustainable solution, leading to widespread adoption and positive feedback.

Even as the pandemic subsided, the company retained a strong market presence. It expanded its product offerings to include a range of sustainable cleaning and hygiene solutions beyond hand sanitisation.

Additional innovations were introduced, such as a solution that allowed customers to order food directly from their tables in restaurants, further enhancing the company's offerings.

This case study underscores the importance of adaptability and responsiveness in the face of changing market conditions. By recognising the need for touchless hygiene solutions and leveraging its existing infrastructure, the company was able to turn challenges into opportunities for growth and positive societal impact.

The company's dedication to sustainability and public health solidified its position as a leader in the hygiene solutions market, demonstrating the effectiveness of strategic pivots in navigating evolving business landscapes.

There are several signs that may indicate the need to pivot your business.

Business

First, declining or stagnant sales and revenue can be a clear signal that your current business model or offerings are no longer resonating with customers.

If you're consistently facing challenges in acquiring new customers or retaining existing ones, it may be time to consider a pivot.

Additionally, customer feedback and market research can provide valuable insights. If you consistently receive feedback that your product or service is not meeting customer needs or that there are emerging market trends you're not addressing, it's a sign that adjustments are necessary.

Another indication is when you encounter unexpected competition or disruptive changes in the industry landscape. If new technologies or competitors emerge, threatening your market position or making your business model obsolete, a pivot may be necessary for survival and growth.

Lastly, internal factors such as a lack of employee engagement or expertise gaps in your team can also point to the need for change. When your business faces any combination of these signs, it's essential to reassess your strategies, offerings, and target market, and consider a pivot to ensure long-term viability and success.

If you choose not to pivot your business despite clear indications for change, several negative consequences can arise.

Business

First and foremost, you risk becoming stagnant or obsolete in the market. By ignoring shifts in customer preferences, emerging technologies, or industry trends, your products or services may lose relevance, resulting in declining sales, dwindling customer base, and ultimately, financial instability.

Your competitors, who adapt and cater to changing market demands, may outperform and overshadow your business, leading to loss of market share and competitive advantage.

Moreover, without a pivot, you may miss out on new opportunities for growth and innovation. Failing to adapt to evolving customer needs or explore emerging markets can limit your business's potential and hinder your ability to stay ahead of the competition.

Additionally, internal issues such as low employee morale and disengagement can arise from the frustration of working within an outdated or ineffective business model. Over time, this can lead to talent attrition, difficulty in attracting top talent, and decreased productivity.

Case Study: Evolution of the Video Rental Industry

During the period from 1985 to 2010, a prominent player in the video rental sector dominated the market with numerous outlets worldwide. This company offered an extensive array of movies and video games for rental, catering to customers' entertainment needs within their homes.

However, the landscape of the entertainment industry underwent a significant transformation with the rise of online streaming and digital media.

Regrettably, the video rental store's inability to pivot and adjust to this evolving terrain marked the beginning of its downfall. Despite early signs indicating the escalating popularity of online movie rentals and streaming services, the store remained firmly committed to its traditional brick-and-mortar retail model, largely overlooking the shift toward digital content consumption.

As online streaming platforms gained momentum, the store's customer base began to dwindle. The allure of convenience, cost-effectiveness, and expansive content libraries provided by streaming services enticed consumers seeking immediate access to a diverse range of entertainment from the comfort of their homes. The company's reliance on physical stores severely restricted its capacity to compete effectively in this emerging digital landscape.

Furthermore, missed opportunities to acquire or establish partnerships with emerging digital platforms further compounded the store's woes. An opportunity arose to acquire a popular streaming service in its infancy, but the company failed to grasp the potential of the online rental and streaming model. This decision further entrenched the store's identity as a dated and resistant participant within the industry.

The retail-centric business model progressively became untenable. The financial strain of maintaining an extensive network of physical outlets, managing inventory, and overseeing rental logistics weighed heavily on the company's finances. As revenue dwindled, the store found itself grappling with accumulating debts and struggling to align with shifting consumer preferences.

Though attempts were made to introduce an independent online rental service and subscription model, these endeavors proved too little, too late. The company's lack of agility and brand recognition hindered its ability to compete with established streaming platforms that had already secured a substantial portion of the market.

In 2010, the company filed for bankruptcy, marking the closure of its remaining outlets and the end of an era in the video rental industry. The store's failure to embrace the digital revolution and adapt its business model culminated in its demise, serving as a poignant example for enterprises that fail to acclimate to the ever-changing dynamics of the market.

This case study underscores the importance of recognising shifts within an industry, embracing innovation, and adapting to evolving consumer preferences. Through its reluctance to pivot and capitalise on emergent technologies, the store forfeited its relevance, market share, and ultimately, its foothold in the entertainment sector.

Accounting

Accounting

Importance of Owners in Financial Management

Directorship and ownership play a crucial role in the financial management and overall success of a small company. The financial decisions made by directors and owners have a significant impact on the company's growth, stability, and ability to weather challenges.

1. Investment in the Future:

Directors and owners need to ensure that the business has access to sufficient capital for investment in future growth opportunities. Adequate funding allows the company to innovate, expand, and remain competitive in the market.

2. Financial Reserves for Early Stages:

Personal reserves available to directors and owners during the initial stages of the business are essential. These reserves act as a safety net to handle unexpected expenses or fluctuations in revenue that can occur in the early months of operation.

3. Long-Term Viability:

Directors and owners should have personal financial stability even in the event of the company's closure. This ensures that their decision-making is aligned with the best interests of the business rather than being driven solely by self-preservation.

Accounting

Envelope Stuffing: Managing Finances Effectively

To ensure effective financial management, directors and owners can utilise the envelope stuffing method, which involves allocating funds into specific accounts for different financial purposes. This method provides several benefits:

1. Clear Allocation of Funds:

Envelope stuffing allows for a clear and organised allocation of funds to specific purposes, such as profits, taxes, operational expenses, and planned projects. This clarity helps directors and owners understand how much money is available for each category.

2. Financial Awareness:

By maintaining separate accounts for different financial aspects, directors and owners can easily track profits, expenses, and tax obligations. This awareness helps in making informed decisions and prevents overestimating available funds due to delayed obligations like VAT.

3. Financial Control:

Having dedicated accounts for various purposes gives directors and owners better control over their finances. It prevents commingling of funds and ensures that money is allocated appropriately, reducing the risk of overspending in one area.

4. Prioritisation and Decision-Making:

Envelope stuffing enables informed decision-making by providing a clear overview of the financial situation. Directors and owners can prioritise projects, allocate resources, and make adjustments based on the availability of funds in each account.

5. Stress Reduction and Informed Choices:

Knowing exactly where the business stands financially reduces uncertainty and stress. Directors and owners can confidently make choices about project investments, resource allocation, and growth strategies.

In conclusion, the active involvement of directors and owners in the financial management of a small company is essential for its success and longevity. By having a solid grasp of the company's financial health, making informed decisions, and employing methods like envelope stuffing, directors and owners can steer the business toward growth, sustainability, and profitability. Effective financial management not only ensures the company's well-being but also reflects responsible stewardship of its resources.

Accounts

As the owner, director, or manager of a company, you must understand your business finances and how to manage them. One of the biggest problems for SMEs and even large businesses is the lack of financial management.

Accounting

Many businesses hire an accountant and expect them to monitor the profits and losses - and then provide advice.

That is a misconception.

An accountant will not monitor your finances, they are there to confirm what you should already know about your financial performance. For example, confirming that you have not made a profit, have only just broken even, how much you are owed, or that you need to pay tax.

If you trust accountants to handle the financial management of the company, there is a big risk that you will have no idea where your business stands financially. This is because you as an owner should be taking action to monitor your cash, understand your profit and loss, and know where your business stands financially, always.

It is important for you to monitor your finances so that your business can prepare for any challenges or opportunities that require investment to grow.

Knowledge of your finances will also help your business survive through events such as COVID and the Cost-of-Living Crisis, as you'll understand how to best manage your cash.

You can seek advice from a financial advisor to help monitor your finances and navigate through hard times.

Accounting

Financial advisors and accountants are two different professions.

As an owner, you need to be agile with your account management and finances. This means being prepared to make a change to your business operations whenever it is necessary for not only survival but growth, whether it's putting a project on hold or purchasing better equipment that will improve efficiency and productivity.

You can only make these necessary changes when you understand how much money you actually have.

Cash Reserves

Maintaining your cash reserves is of utmost importance, not just from a financial standpoint, but also for the psychological well-being of your management team. While it's truly inspiring to work under a leader who motivates the team, it can be disheartening when their visionary ideas lack the financial backing to materialise.

The awareness of cash reserves profoundly impacts your workforce. There are distinct signs that become evident when financial concerns arise, affecting the morale and performance of your team members:

Delayed Invoice Payments: Invoices taking longer to be settled than usual.

Missed Allowance Payments: Instances where allowances or reimbursements are not met on time.

Accounting

Challenges in Salary Negotiations: Difficulties arising during negotiations for salary adjustments or increments.

Absence of New Product Lines: The absence of new products or services being introduced.

Decreased Invoice Activity: A noticeable reduction in the frequency of invoices being generated.

Lack of Future Planning: The absence of a clear roadmap or strategy for the future.

These signs do not go unnoticed. The perceptive members of your team will be quick to pick up on such indications, and this awareness can have cascading effects. Valued individuals within the organisation might start exploring opportunities elsewhere, seeking more stable environments.

In an effort to safeguard against such circumstances, we recommend maintaining a reserve equivalent to three months' worth of salaries.

This safety net is in place to address potential crisis and facilitate a structured and orderly process, should the need for redundancy or a controlled shutdown arise.

It's crucial to clarify that your goal is to never encounter such a scenario. Nevertheless, we recognise that unforeseen challenges can arise in the course of running a business.

Accounting

Completing Projections

In the realm of financial planning and decision-making, projections stand as a key tool to envision potential outcomes and plan for the future. However, it is important to approach projections with a clear understanding of their nature and limitations.

At best, projections are an educated guess - where analysis, historical data, and industry insights come together to formulate a plausible trajectory. Yet, even within an educated guess, an element of chance is present, reminding us that projections, while based on solid groundwork, remain subject to the changing financial landscape.

On the other end of the spectrum lies the possibility of an uneducated lie – a projection lacking substance, driven by hasty assumptions or wishful thinking. Such projections, while tempting in their optimism, can lead to misguided decisions and detrimental outcomes.

Between these two extremes, a third avenue occurs - an educated lie, crafted to align with a desired investment narrative. This manoeuvre involves shaping projections to meet predetermined objectives, painting a picture that appeals to potential investors or secures further funding.

Accounting

Designing and Completing an Educated Business Projection:

Creating an effective business projection involves careful analysis and forecasting of key financial metrics. Here's a step-by-step guide to help you design and complete a projection for your business:

Gather Historical Data: Start by collecting historical financial data from your business. This includes past revenue, expenses, profit margins, and cash flow. The more data you have, the better you can identify trends and patterns.

Define Assumptions: Clearly outline the assumptions that will drive your projections. These could be related to sales growth rates, cost of goods sold, operating expenses, market trends, or any other relevant factors. Base these assumptions on market research, historical data, and insights from industry experts.

Build Revenue Projections: Use the assumptions to forecast your future revenue. Depending on your business, you can break down revenue projections by product lines, customer segments, or geographic regions. Be realistic and consider various scenarios, including best-case, worst-case, and moderate projections.

Estimate Expenses: Project your operating expenses, including rent, utilities, salaries, marketing costs, and any other relevant expenditures. Again, consider different scenarios and potential cost-cutting measures.

Accounting

Calculate Gross Profit and Net Income: Subtract your projected cost of goods sold (COGS) from revenue to determine gross profit. Then deduct operating expenses to calculate net income.

Assess Cash Flow: Cash flow is crucial for business survival. Analyse your projected cash flow by considering the timing of revenue collection and expense payments. Identify potential cash flow gaps and plan accordingly.

Monitor Key Metrics: Use key performance indicators (KPIs) to track the success of your projection. This might include customer acquisition cost, customer lifetime value, customer churn rate, etc. Regularly review your actual performance against projections and adjust your strategy as needed.

Completing a business projection for a startup involves a slightly different approach due to the unique challenges and uncertainties startups often face. Here's a modified step-by-step guide specifically tailored for completing a business projection as a startup:

Understand Your Business Model: Clearly define your startup's business model. Understand how your product or service will create value, who your target customers are, and how you plan to generate revenue.

Set Realistic Goals: Start with achievable goals. While ambition is important, being overly optimistic in your projections can lead to unrealistic expectations. Base your initial projections on conservative estimates.

Accounting

Validate Assumptions: Since startups have limited historical data, focus on validating your assumptions. Conduct market research, surveys, and competitor analysis to gather insights that support your projections.

Create Multiple Scenarios: Develop different scenarios, including a base case, best-case, and worst-case scenario. This demonstrates your understanding of potential outcomes and shows investors that you're prepared for uncertainties.

Focus on Key Metrics: Identify the core metrics that matter most for your startup's growth. These might include customer acquisition cost (CAC), customer lifetime value (CLTV), conversion rates, churn rates, and viral coefficient. Tailor your projections to these metrics.

Build a Detailed Sales Plan: Outline your sales strategy. Break down your sales projections by channels, customer segments, or geographic regions. Describe how you'll acquire customers and the expected conversion rates.

Consider Funding Rounds: If your startup plans to raise funding, incorporate the timing and amount of funding rounds into your projections. Outline how the infusion of capital will impact your operations and growth trajectory.

Accounting

Address Operational Costs: Estimate your startup's operational expenses. Consider costs related to product development, marketing, hiring, office space, technology, and any other relevant areas.

Cash Flow Management: Pay special attention to your startup's cash flow. Startups often experience cash constraints, so project your cash inflows and outflows on a monthly basis to identify potential bottlenecks.

Iterative Approach: Recognise that your projections will evolve over time. As your startup gains traction and collects more data, refine your projections and assumptions. Regularly update your projections to align with your actual performance.

Seek Professional Advice: If you're unsure about certain aspects of financial projections, consider seeking advice from a financial advisor, mentor, or consultant with experience in startup finance.

Be Transparent: When presenting your projections to potential investors or stakeholders, be transparent about your assumptions, methodologies, and the inherent risks associated with a startup venture.

As your startup progresses, your projections will serve as a valuable tool for measuring performance and making strategic decisions.

Accounting

Developing a Cash Runway Plan for the Next 6 Months:

A cash runway plan helps you understand how long your business can operate before running out of funds. To create a cash runway plan for the next 6 months, follow these steps:

Determine Current Cash Position: Begin with the amount of cash your business currently has available.

Forecast Cash Inflows: Estimate the expected cash inflows over the next 6 months. This includes revenue from sales, investments, loans, or any other sources of cash.

Forecast Cash Outflows: Project all anticipated cash outflows, including operating expenses, loan repayments, inventory purchases, and any other cash disbursements.

Calculate Burn Rate: The burn rate is the rate at which your business is consuming cash to cover expenses. Divide the projected cash outflows by the number of months to get the monthly burn rate.

Determine Cash Runway: Divide your current cash position by the monthly burn rate to find the number of months your cash will last. This is your cash runway.

Accounting

Identify Cash Management Strategies: If your cash runway is less than 6 months, consider implementing strategies to extend it. These may include reducing expenses, renegotiating contracts, raising capital through investments or loans, or accelerating revenue generation through marketing efforts.

Review and Revise: Regularly review and update your cash runway plan as circumstances change. Reevaluate assumptions and adjust projections accordingly to stay proactive in managing your business's financial health.

By designing an effective business projection and developing a cash runway plan, you can make informed decisions and ensure the financial stability and growth of your business in the face of uncertainty.

Let's consider two scenarios: one where a business follows the process of developing a Cash Runway Plan for the next 6 months, and another where a business doesn't follow the process.

Scenario 1: Business Follows the Cash Runway Plan Process

Business: XYZ Tech Solutions (a software startup)

Determine Current Cash Position: XYZ Tech Solutions begins with £100,000 in available cash.

Accounting

Forecast Cash Inflows: The company estimates £50,000 in monthly revenue from software sales and subscription services, totalling £300,000 over the next 6 months.

Forecast Cash Outflows: XYZ projects monthly operating expenses of £30,000, which include salaries, marketing, and office rent. Additionally, they expect a loan repayment of £20,000 over the 6 months.

Calculate Burn Rate: Monthly burn rate = (£30,000 + £20,000) / 6 = £8,333.33.

Determine Cash Runway: Cash runway = £100,000 / £8,333.33 ≈ 12 months.

Identify Cash Management Strategies: With a 12-month cash runway, XYZ Tech Solutions feels confident in their financial position. They continue to focus on revenue generation and product improvement.

Review and Revise: Every month, XYZ reviews their actual cash inflows and outflows. They find that revenue is slightly higher than projected, and expenses are lower due to some cost-saving measures. They adjust their projections accordingly.

Scenario 2: Business Doesn't Follow the Cash Runway Plan Process

Business: ABC Clothing Store (a retail startup)

Determine Current Cash Position: ABC Clothing Store begins with £50,000 in available cash.

Accounting

Forecast Cash Inflows: The company expects revenue from clothing sales and estimates £20,000 in monthly sales, totalling £120,000 over the next 6 months.

Forecast Cash Outflows: ABC projects monthly operating expenses of £25,000, including rent, salaries, and inventory costs. They also plan to invest £10,000 in a marketing campaign.

Calculate Burn Rate: Monthly burn rate = (£25,000 + £10,000) / 6 = £5,833.33.

Determine Cash Runway: Cash runway = £50,000 / £5,833.33 ≈ 8.6 months.

Identify Cash Management Strategies: Realising their cash runway is below 6 months, ABC Clothing Store decides to delay the marketing campaign and cut some operational costs. They do not consider raising additional capital.

Consequences: After 4 months, ABC Clothing Store faces unexpected supply chain disruptions due to the pandemic. Their sales drop significantly, and their cash position quickly dwindles. They struggle to pay rent and salaries, leading to financial distress. Without a clear plan, they are forced to make hasty decisions to survive.

In Scenario 2, where ABC Clothing Store's cash runway is less than 6 months, they should have taken proactive steps to extend their cash runway and improve their financial stability. Here's what they could have done:

Accounting

Immediate Cost Reduction: Identify areas where expenses can be cut without significantly affecting operations. This might include renegotiating contracts, reducing discretionary spending, and optimising inventory management.

Delay Non-Essential Spending: Postpone or scale back non-essential expenditures, such as marketing campaigns or expansion plans, until the financial situation stabilises.

Explore Alternative Financing: Consider seeking short-term financing options, such as a line of credit or a small business loan, to inject additional capital into the business and extend the cash runway.

Accelerate Revenue Generation: Focus on strategies to increase sales and revenue. This might involve running targeted promotions, introducing new product lines, or exploring partnerships to drive customer acquisition.

Inventory Management: Efficiently manage inventory levels to avoid overstocking or stockouts. Analyse sales data to determine which products are most popular and adjust inventory orders accordingly.

Customer Engagement: Strengthen relationships with existing customers to encourage repeat business. Implement loyalty programs or discounts to incentivise purchases and enhance customer retention.

Accounting

Cash Flow Monitoring: Establish a rigorous cash flow monitoring process. Regularly review cash inflows and outflows, and update the cash runway calculations based on actual performance.

Scenario Planning: Develop contingency plans for various scenarios, including further disruptions or changes in market conditions. Outline specific actions to take if certain events occur.

Communication with Stakeholders: Keep stakeholders, including employees, suppliers, and investors, informed about the financial challenges and the steps being taken to address them. Transparent communication can foster support and understanding.

Seek Professional Advice: Consult with financial advisors or business mentors who have experience in managing financial crisis. They can provide valuable insights and guidance on navigating challenging situations.

Long-Term Sustainability: While focusing on short-term cash flow is crucial, ABC Clothing Store should also assess their business model and long-term sustainability. Consider diversifying revenue streams, exploring e-commerce options, or adapting the product mix to align with changing customer preferences.

Reevaluate and Adjust: Continuously monitor the effectiveness of the strategies implemented. If conditions change, be prepared to adjust the approach accordingly.

Accounting

By taking these steps, ABC Clothing Store could have increased their chances of extending their cash runway, navigating the financial challenges, and positioning the business for long-term success. It's important to remain agile and responsive during uncertain times, making informed decisions based on a clear understanding of the business's financial health.

Actually Making a Real Profit

Small businesses encounter significant hurdles on their journey towards profitability and sustainability. There are several ways in which small businesses may struggle to generate consistent profits and maintain long-term viability. From undercompensated directors to mismanaged capital, from short-term cost-cutting measures to questionable staffing practices, these challenges can collectively impede a business's ability to thrive in a competitive marketplace. Understanding these pitfalls can shed light on the complexities small businesses navigate and underscore the importance of strategic decision-making and financial planning for their success.

Undercompensated Directors: When small business directors or owners are not fully compensated for their work, it can lead to burnout and demotivation. This can hinder business growth and sustainability as key decision-makers are not adequately focused on driving the company forward.

Accounting

Proposed Solution: Hire operational managers to handle day-to-day operations, allowing directors to focus on the future and strategic decision-making. Allocate appropriate compensation to directors for their efforts, aligning incentives with the company's growth and profitability.

Undercapitalisation: When businesses are not adequately capitalised, they may struggle to cover operational costs, invest in growth, or weather unexpected financial challenges. Relying on limited capital can limit a business's ability to seize opportunities and navigate economic downturns. Undercapitalisation can be caused by imbalanced cash inflows and outflows, which can become problematic over time. In other cases, undercapitalisation describes a situation where a company simply needs more funds than it has or can access in order to grow.

Proposed Solution: Develop a budget aligned with the business plan that can be used to manage cash inflows and spending. Regularly monitor and analyse any deviations from the budget to ensure that the business remains adequately funded.

Mismanaged Capital Injection: If directors inject capital into the business at rates below market standards or without a clear repayment plan, it can create financial imbalances and potentially strain the business relationship. This can lead to issues if the business cannot generate enough profits to repay the borrowed capital.

Accounting

Proposed Solution: Establish clear terms for capital injections from directors, including repayment plans and interest rates aligned with market standards. This promotes transparency and ensures that the business is not burdened by unsustainable debt.

Capital Flow for Financing: Relying solely on capital flow for financing (revenue from operations) may limit a business's ability to grow quickly or respond to market changes. This can hinder expansion plans and limit investment in critical areas like marketing, technology, and talent.

Proposed Solution: Diversify financing sources beyond capital flow from operations. Consider seeking external funding, creating a contingency fund, or exploring strategic partnerships that can infuse additional capital and support growth initiatives.

Selling Capital Assets: Selling off capital assets, such as buildings or equipment, to cover operational losses or short-term financial challenges can reduce a business's long-term capacity to generate profits. This approach can erode the business's ability to serve customers and compete effectively.

Proposed Solution: Prioritise maintaining key capital assets necessary for business operations. If asset sales are necessary, ensure they are part of a well-defined strategy and do not compromise the business's core capabilities or long-term growth potential.

Accounting

Reducing Stock Levels: While reducing stock levels temporarily may help manage cash flow, it can lead to stockouts, missed sales opportunities, and dissatisfied customers. Long-term reduction in inventory levels can harm the business's ability to meet customer demands.

Proposed Solution: Implement an inventory management system to optimise stock levels based on demand and sales patterns. This ensures that the business can meet customer demands without overspending on excessive inventory.

Short-Term Cost-Cutting: Implementing short-term cost-cutting measures, such as reducing staff levels, can impact service quality, productivity, and employee morale. If these measures are not sustainable or strategic, they may hinder the business's long-term growth.

Proposed Solution: Instead of abrupt cost-cutting, focus on efficiency improvements and process optimisations to achieve sustainable reductions in operational expenses. Invest in staff training and technology to enhance productivity.

Staff Recruitment and Turnover: Allowing for high turnover, whatever the reason, may initially seem cost-effective, but it's essential to recognise the long-term drawbacks. High turnover can lead to higher recruitment and training costs, disrupt operations, and harm team relationships.

Accounting

Proposed Solution: Prioritise employee development, offer competitive wages, and create an environment where team members feel valued and engaged. This commitment to fair treatment not only reduces turnover but also cultivates a dedicated and motivated workforce, contributing to sustainable growth and success.

Lack of Financial Planning: Failing to develop a clear financial plan that considers both short-term and long-term goals can lead to inconsistent cash flow, overspending, and lack of funds for growth opportunities. Without proper financial planning, a business may struggle to allocate resources effectively.

Proposed Solution: Develop a financial plan that encompasses short-term and long-term goals. Regularly review and adjust the plan to reflect changing market conditions, business performance, and growth opportunities.

Dependence on Owner's Expertise: If a small business relies heavily on the expertise of the owner without building a strong team or documenting processes, it can create a bottleneck in decision-making and hinder the business's ability to grow beyond the owner's capacity.

Proposed Solution: Cultivate a capable management team to complement the owner's expertise. Document processes and delegate responsibilities to team members, enabling the business to operate smoothly even in the owner's absence.

Accounting

In summary, small businesses may face challenges that hinder their ability to generate consistent profits and achieve long-term sustainability. These challenges often stem from issues related to capital, financial planning, operational decisions, and talent management. Developing a well-rounded business strategy, focusing on sustainable growth, and making informed financial decisions are crucial steps to overcoming these challenges.

By adopting a strategic and proactive approach to financial management, resource allocation, and talent development, small businesses can enhance their capacity to thrive.

Increasing Profits

Incorporating the following methods into your business strategy can help small businesses increase profits and create a foundation for sustainable growth. It's important to regularly analyse your business performance, adapt to changing market dynamics, and remain agile in your approach to ensure long-term success.

Improving Productivity through Software and Automation: Implementing software solutions and automation tools can significantly enhance productivity by streamlining processes, reducing manual errors, and freeing up valuable time for teams.

Accounting

Examples include customer relationship management (CRM) systems, project management tools, inventory management software, and automated marketing platforms. Automation can also help with tasks like invoicing, data entry, and customer support, allowing employees to focus on higher-value activities.

Increasing Sales Volume with Existing Resources: Optimising sales strategies and tactics can lead to higher sales volume without necessarily requiring additional resources. Consider techniques such as cross-selling and upselling to encourage customers to purchase more or upgrade to premium products or services. Offering bundle deals or discounts for multiple purchases can also incentivise customers to buy more.

Repeat Business through Positive Word of Mouth: Delivering exceptional products or services and providing outstanding customer experiences can lead to positive word of mouth, which is a powerful driver of repeat business. Encourage satisfied customers to leave reviews, testimonials, and referrals. Building strong relationships with customers by maintaining open communication and addressing their needs can foster loyalty and increase the likelihood of repeat purchases.

Introducing New Revenue Streams: Diversifying your offerings can open up new revenue streams. For instance, if you're a retail business, you could start offering online sales or subscription services. If you provide services, consider adding complementary services that align with your expertise.

Identify opportunities to leverage your existing customer base and expertise to expand your product or service offerings.

Enhancing Customer Experience: Investing in exceptional customer service and creating a seamless and personalised experience can differentiate your business and lead to customer loyalty. Anticipate customer needs, provide quick and helpful support, and actively seek feedback to continuously improve your offerings. A positive customer experience can lead to repeat business, referrals, and long-term customer relationships.

Pricing Optimisation: Regularly review and adjust your pricing strategy based on market trends, competitor pricing, and customer willingness to pay. Conduct market research to understand the value your products or services provide to customers and adjust your pricing accordingly. Implementing dynamic pricing strategies or offering tiered pricing options can also attract different customer segments.

Effective Marketing and Branding: Invest in targeted marketing campaigns to reach your ideal customers. Utilise digital marketing channels such as social media, search engine optimisation (SEO), and content marketing to increase your online visibility. Build a strong brand identity that resonates with your target audience, and consistently communicate your unique value proposition.

Accounting

Team Training and Development: Empower your teams with the necessary skills and knowledge to excel in their roles. Teams can enhance customer interactions, improve efficiency, and contribute to a positive work environment. A motivated and skilled workforce can lead to increased customer satisfaction and higher sales.

Strategic Partnerships: Collaborating with other businesses or industry partners can expand your reach and customer base. Identify synergies with businesses that offer complementary products or services and explore opportunities for joint promotions, co-branded initiatives, or cross-marketing campaigns.

Incoming Profits

Confirming where your profits are coming from and focusing on these areas is a fundamental strategy for optimising business performance and maximising revenue. This involves identifying and prioritising products, services, or segments of your business that contribute the most to your bottom line. Let's delve into this concept using the restaurant industry and the example of an automatic coffee shop and a traditional coffee shop:

In the restaurant trade, understanding the profitability of different menu items is crucial for making informed decisions.

Accounting

The example of an automatic coffee shop and a traditional coffee shop demonstrates how businesses can strategically manage their offerings to capitalise on high-margin products while also considering customer preferences and operational efficiency.

Automatic: An automatic coffee shop uses automatic bean-to-cup machines for its coffee preparation. While these machines may have higher upfront costs and training requirements, they offer consistent quality and speed, resulting in quicker service. An automatic coffee shop focuses on the coffee segment, a high-margin product that drives a significant portion of its revenue. This approach aligns with its branding as a premium coffee provider and appeals to customers seeking convenience and a consistent experience.

Traditional: A traditional coffee shop, on the other hand, uses traditional coffee machines. While these machines may require more training and potentially lead to slightly longer service times, the traditional coffee shop emphasises the artisanal aspect of coffee preparation. They target customers who value a more traditional and personalised coffee experience. Despite potential operational complexities, the traditional coffee shop maintains a high-margin strategy by capitalising on customer preferences for quality and uniqueness.

In both cases, understanding the profitability and appeal of their respective offerings allows these coffee shops to optimise their business models:

Accounting

Profit Focus: By recognising that coffee is a high-margin product, both prioritise coffee sales. This includes emphasising product quality, consistency, and efficient delivery to maintain profitability.

Customer Preferences: While they have different approaches, they align their strategies with what their target customers value. The automatic coffee shop offers convenience and consistency, catering to busy customers who want their coffee quickly. The traditional coffee shop appeals to those who appreciate a more personalised experience.

Operational Efficiency: The use of automatic machines streamlines the coffee-making process, reducing service time and potentially increasing customer turnover. The traditional approach offers a unique selling point, even if it requires more training and slightly longer service times.

Training and Investment: Both invest in training to ensure their staff can deliver high-quality products efficiently. While the training costs may differ, they recognise the importance of skilled and knowledgeable employees in maintaining customer satisfaction.

Ultimately, the key takeaway is the importance of aligning your business strategy with your most profitable areas while considering customer preferences and operational efficiency.

By focusing on these areas, you can create a more targeted and effective approach to resource allocation, marketing, and customer engagement, leading to sustained growth and profitability. Regular analysis and adaptation based on profitability insights ensure that your business remains agile and competitive in a dynamic market.

Linking Your Goals to Your Numbers

Profit represents revenue over expenses, indicating the financial success of your business operations. It's the fuel that drives growth, innovation, and the ability to weather economic challenges. Profits enable reinvestment, expansion, talent acquisition, and technology adoption. They are an indicator of your business's efficiency, competitiveness, and value creation. For management, recognising the significance of profits goes beyond the numbers—it's about ensuring the longevity of the organisation.

Profitability should be tightly linked to your business goals and strategies. Every financial decision, from pricing strategies to cost control, should be aligned with the overarching objectives of your business. Whether it's increasing market share, launching new products, or entering new markets, profits play a central role in funding these initiatives. Effective management involves using profitability insights to guide resource allocation, prioritise projects, and make strategic choices that advance your long-term vision.

Accounting

Even profitable ventures can fail if cash isn't managed effectively. Profits on paper don't guarantee survival if there's a gap between when money comes in and when expenses are due. Businesses need cash to cover operating costs, pay employees, service debt, invest in growth, and handle unforeseen challenges. A lack of available cash can lead to missed opportunities, strained relationships with suppliers, and even bankruptcy. Management's role includes monitoring cash flow, managing working capital, and ensuring the business maintains adequate liquidity.

Effective management requires integrating these three critical elements: profits, goals, and cash. It's not enough to focus solely on generating profits without a clear purpose. Goals provide direction and context to profitability efforts. Likewise, cash management must be a constant consideration, ensuring that profits translate into tangible resources to support ongoing operations and strategic initiatives. Effective financial management involves finding the right balance between reinvesting profits, servicing debt, maintaining reserves, and securing the liquidity needed for day-to-day operations.

In summary, profitability is the cornerstone of a thriving business, but it must be understood and managed within the context of your goals and the availability of cash.

Accounting

Effective management involves recognising the interconnectedness of these factors and making informed decisions that drive profitability while ensuring the business remains financially resilient. By maintaining this balance and aligning financial decisions with your overarching vision, management can navigate challenges, seize opportunities, and pave the way for sustainable success.

Business Possibilities

It is crucial to evaluate the potential and sustainability of your business – essentially, how far can you envision leading your business? To accomplish this, you should analyse the risks associated with your business idea.

For instance, can you expand in into additional markets? What kind of relationship do you want to establish with customers? Are there additional revenue streams you can explore?

This is why there must be the development of a Business Viability Model. This tool is especially useful for start-up management. With a Business Viability Model, owners can refer to the document to understand the business strategy and angle, and most importantly work our whether their business idea is viable. The model allows them to evaluate the business ideas viability, identify potential gaps or weaknesses, and make informed decisions to refine their strategy for long-term success.

Accounting

The canvas helps ensure that all aspects of the business are considered and aligned, leading to a clearer understanding of whether the business idea is sustainable and viable over the long term.

The model ensures you consider these key factors:

Products/Services: This element defines what you are building for the customers and the benefits provided.

- What products are we offering to the customer?
- Which customer problems are we helping solve?
- What value do we deliver to the customer's life?

Audience: This element defines customer segment specifics, as customers should be divided into segments by their various needs and characteristics.

- Who are our customer segments?
- What type of relationship do we hope to establish with the customer?
- How do we retain customers and repeat business?
- How do we grow customers?

Routes & Revenue Paths: This element defines how your product will be delivered to the target audience. You should also define the method by which your company will generate income from each customer segment.

- Which channels do customers want to be reached?

- How are we reaching them? Which work best? Which are most cost-efficient?
- What are the customers willing to pay for the product? What do they currently pay?
- How are they currently paying? How would they prefer to pay?
- How much does each revenue stream contribute to overall revenue?
- What are the monetisation plans?

Resources & Support: This element defines what assets and supplies are needed through the development and delivery of your product. You should also add the key partners, shareholders, suppliers, and support essential to the delivery of the entire business model and product.

- What are the most important resources?
- What teams support the business model?
- Who are our partners, suppliers, and shareholders?
- What resources are we acquiring from partners?
- Which activities do these partners help us perform?

Activities & Expenses: This element identifies the most important tasks a business needs to conduct for the model to function effectively. You should also define the cost and expense of pursuing the model.

Accounting

- What important activities does the business need to perform for the model to function effectively?
- What are the costs of the resources and activities? Including support activities.
- Which resources are the most expensive?
- Which activities are the most expensive?
- What is the cost of pursuing partnerships?

CAC & Repeat Business Costs: CAC stands for Customer Acquisition Cost and refers to the cost of acquiring a new customer.

It is the total amount of money spent to acquire a new customer, divided by the number of customers acquired.

Repeat business costs refer to the expenses that a business incurs to retain existing customers and generate repeat sales.

Level of Profitability: The amount of money a business is making after subtracting all of its expenses from its revenue.

Route-to-Market Timeframe & Key Milestones: Route-to-market milestones refer to the timebound key steps or stages that a company must go through in order to successfully bring a product or service to market.

Products/Services:	Audience:	Routes & Revenue Paths:	Resources & Support:	Activities & Expenses:
This element defines what you are building for the customers and the benefits provided.	This element defines customer segment specifics, as customers should be divided into segments by their various needs and characteristics.	This element defines how your product will be delivered to the target audience. You should also define the method by which your company will generate income from each audience segment.	This element defines what assets and supplies are needed through the development and delivery of your product. You should also add the key partners, suppliers, and support essential to the delivery of the entire Business Model and product.	This identifies the most important tasks a business needs to carry out for the model to function effectively. You should also define the cost and expense of pursuing the Business Model.
What products and services are we offering to the customer segments?	Who are our customer segments?	Through which channels do our customer segments want to be reached?		What important tasks and activities does the business need to carry out for the model to function effectively?
Which of our customer's problems are we helping to solve?	What type of relationship do we hope to establish with the customer?	How are we reaching them now? Which ones work best? Which ones are most cost-efficient?	What are the most important resources in our business model?	What are the costs of your resources and activities? Including support activities.
What value do we deliver to the customer's life?	How do we retain customers and ensure repeat business?	What are the customers willing to pay for the product? What do they currently pay?	What teams support the business model? Including support & sales.	Which resources are the most expensive?
	How do we grow customers?	How are they currently paying? How would they prefer to pay?	Who are our partners & suppliers?	Which activities are the most expensive?
		How much does each revenue stream contribute to overall revenue?	What resources are we acquiring from these partners?	What is the cost of pursuing partnerships?
		What are the monetisation plans?	Which activities do these partners help us perform?	

CAC & Repeat Business Costs:

Level of Profitability:
The amount of money a business is making after subtracting all of its expenses from its revenue.

CAC stands for "Customer Acquisition Cost," and refers to the cost of acquiring a new customer. It's the total amount of money spent to acquire a new customer, divided by the number of customers acquired. Repeat business costs refer to the expenses that a business incurs to retain existing customers and generate repeat sales.

What is the cost of acquiring customers?
What is the cost of retaining customers?
What is the cost of growing customers?

Route-to-Market Timeframe & Key Milestones:
Route-to-market milestones refer to the key steps or stages that a company must go through in order to successfully bring a product or service to market.

Accounting

Continuous Improvement in Profits

Understanding and implementing methods to improve profits is a crucial aspect of running a successful business. While there are numerous strategies available, some are more evident, while others are less conventional yet equally effective.

Obvious Methods:

Increase Product Lines: Expanding your product or service offerings can attract a wider customer base and encourage existing customers to make additional purchases. Diversifying your product lines can lead to increased sales and higher overall profits.

Increase the Number of Customers: Attracting new customers through effective marketing and customer engagement efforts can boost revenue. Acquiring new customers while retaining existing ones can contribute significantly to profit growth.

Increase Advertising to Expand Customer Base: Investing in targeted advertising and marketing campaigns can increase brand visibility, attract more customers, and drive higher sales, ultimately leading to improved profits.

Accounting

Less Obvious Methods:

Adding Extensions (Add-Ons): Offering add-on products or services that complement the main offering can increase the average transaction value. These extras provide additional value to customers and lead to higher profits per sale.

Product Line Separation (Bundle and Unbundle): Similar to how budget airlines offer optional services separately, businesses can unbundle their product lines and charge customers for specific features or components. This allows customers to customise their purchases while maximising profit potential.

Extras Features with Charges: Offering premium features or enhancements for an additional fee can entice customers to upgrade and pay more for enhanced value. This approach is commonly seen in software subscriptions and premium memberships.

These less obvious methods often require a deeper understanding of consumer behaviour and creative thinking to implement effectively. They focus on extracting additional value from each customer interaction and transaction. By adopting these strategies, businesses can enhance their revenue streams and improve overall profitability.

It's important to note that the effectiveness of each method can vary based on factors such as industry, target audience, and market trends.

Accounting

Businesses should carefully analyse their unique circumstances and consider a combination of both obvious and less obvious methods to create a strategy for boosting profits.

Regular monitoring, analysis, and adaptation are essential to ensure that the chosen methods are delivering the desired results. By continually seeking innovative ways to increase profits, businesses can maintain a competitive edge and achieve sustained growth over the long term.

A well-known budget airline employs various pricing strategies, including add-on and bundling/unbundling methods, to enhance its revenue and profitability.

1. Add-On Method: In-Flight Services

The airline offers a range of in-flight services that passengers can add to their basic ticket purchases. These add-ons provide customers with the option to personalise their flying experience and pay for only the services they value.

Examples of in-flight add-ons offered include:

Seat Selection: Passengers can choose their preferred seat in advance for a fee. This option allows travellers to secure seats with extra legroom, near the front of the plane, or with faster exit access.

Additional Baggage Allowance: Passengers can purchase extra baggage allowance if they need to carry more luggage than the standard allowance.

Speedy Boarding: For a fee, passengers can enjoy priority boarding, allowing them to board the aircraft before other passengers and secure overhead storage space for their belongings.

In-Flight Meals and Snacks: The airline offers a selection of meals, snacks, and beverages for purchase during the flight. Passengers have the choice to buy food and drinks that suit their preferences.

2. Bundling/Unbundling Method: Flexi Fare

The airline also employs a bundling/unbundling strategy through its "Flexi Fare" option. With this offering, passengers can choose a higher-priced Flexi Fare ticket, which includes a package of benefits such as:

Free seat selection.

Unlimited date changes without additional fees.

Additional cabin baggage allowance.

Fast-track security at select airports.

By bundling these benefits together, the airline appeals to travellers seeking flexibility and added perks, especially business travellers or those who prioritise convenience.

Accounting

This approach contrasts with the unbundled standard fare, where passengers pay only for the basic flight ticket and can then choose to add individual services, like seat selection or baggage allowance, for an extra cost.

The bundling/unbundling method allows the airline to cater to different customer segments based on their preferences and willingness to pay for added conveniences. Passengers can select the fare type that aligns with their needs, providing them with the flexibility to customise their travel experience while generating additional revenue for the airline.

In summary, the airline strategically utilises add-on services and bundling/unbundling methods to generate additional revenue streams and meet the diverse needs of its passengers. These pricing strategies allow the airline to offer both budget-friendly options and enhanced services, thereby contributing to its overall profitability in a competitive market.

Tax and Payment Delays

There are several different business taxes that are paid on a delay. This simply means that there is a delay in when a payment will be made.

Payroll taxes are paid on a Monthly or Quarterly basis. Corporation Tax is paid 9 months and 1 day after the end of the accounting period. VAT payments are due one month after the end of the accounting period (VAT).

It's important for businesses to think about tax and payment delays for a few reasons.

Firstly, it helps you manage your money effectively by preparing for delays and making sure you have enough cash to cover expenses and bills.

Secondly, it allows you to plan ahead and make realistic predictions about finances, so you can see any potential problems and figure out how to deal with them.

Lastly, businesses need to follow the rules when it comes to paying taxes, or else you could have to pay fines.

Tax Planning

Clear tax planning is a critical aspect of financial management for businesses. It involves making informed decisions and implementing strategies to optimise a company's tax liability while ensuring compliance with tax laws and regulations. Effective tax planning goes beyond just minimising taxes; it also takes into account the company's financial goals, cash flow management, and overall business strategy.

1. Maximising Tax Efficiency:

Strategic tax planning allows businesses to take advantage of legal tax incentives, deductions, and credits to reduce their tax liability.

In the example of capital spending before the end of the tax year, businesses can accelerate expenditures on assets that qualify for depreciation or other tax benefits. By doing so, they can effectively reduce their taxable income, which in turn lowers the amount of corporate tax owed. This helps preserve more of the company's profits and ensures that funds are allocated efficiently.

2. Managing Cash Flow:

Proper tax planning helps businesses avoid unexpected cash flow shortages. Without careful consideration of tax obligations, a company might find itself short of funds when it's time to make urgent payments, seize opportunities, or cover operational expenses. By anticipating tax liabilities and planning for them in advance, businesses can set aside funds or arrange financing to meet their financial obligations without compromising their operations or growth plans.

3. Timing of Invoicing:

Delaying invoicing until after the tax period can be a deliberate tax planning strategy. By doing this, businesses can potentially defer recognising income until the following tax year, which might result in lower tax liabilities for the current year. This approach can provide businesses with more control over their taxable income, allowing them to manage their tax liability effectively.

4. Strategic Resource Allocation:

Effective tax planning enables businesses to allocate resources, such as capital expenditures or investments, in a manner that aligns with their financial goals and tax strategy. Businesses can strategically time major financial decisions to optimise tax benefits, contributing to long-term financial stability and growth.

5. Compliance and Avoidance of Penalties:

Clear tax planning helps businesses stay compliant with tax laws and regulations. Failing to plan and accurately report taxes can lead to costly penalties, audits, and legal issues. By having a well-structured tax planning strategy, businesses can minimise the risk of non-compliance and associated financial repercussions.

In essence, clear tax planning is essential for businesses to ensure that they are not only minimising their tax burden but also strategically managing their finances to support growth, cash flow, and operational needs. Effective tax planning requires careful analysis, collaboration with financial experts or tax advisors, and alignment with the overall business strategy. It empowers businesses to make informed decisions that contribute to their financial health and long-term success.

Accounting

Understand Profitability Excluding Cost Tax

Understanding profitability is a fundamental aspect of sound financial management for any business. It provides crucial insights into the health of the business, informs decision-making, and helps chart a course for sustainable growth. However, understanding profitability goes beyond just looking at revenue and expenses on the surface level. It requires an analysis that considers various factors, including the impact of taxes like VAT (Value Added Tax), corporate tax, and employment taxes.

1. Accurate Reflection of Financial Health: Removing VAT, corporate tax, and employment taxes from your financial calculations provides a clearer picture of your business's true profitability. These taxes are obligations that must be paid to the government, and excluding them reveals the amount of revenue actually available for reinvestment, expansion, and other strategic initiatives. Ignoring these taxes could lead to inaccurate assessments of your business's financial health.

2. Planning and Decision-Making: By accurately understanding your profitability after taxes, you can make more informed decisions about pricing, spending, and resource allocation. Knowing your actual net income empowers you to set realistic targets, create achievable budgets, and allocate resources effectively to drive growth and optimise operations.

3. Sustainable Financial Management: Excluding taxes from your profitability analysis helps you assess whether your business operations are generating sustainable profits over the long term. Businesses that ignore taxes might overestimate their profitability and make decisions based on unreliable financial data, which can lead to financial instability in the future.

4. Cash Flow Management: Understanding your true profitability is essential for managing cash flow effectively. Accurately accounting for tax obligations helps you plan for the timing of tax payments, preventing cash flow crisis when taxes become due. Proper cash flow management ensures you have sufficient funds to meet financial obligations while maintaining day-to-day operations.

5. Tax Planning and Compliance: Removing taxes from profitability analysis also highlights the importance of tax planning. It's essential to factor in tax obligations when estimating future expenses and setting aside funds for tax payments. Failing to do so could lead to financial strain or even penalties for non-compliance.

6. Informed Investment Decisions: When considering investments or expansion opportunities, understanding your true profitability allows you to assess the viability of these ventures more accurately. Investments should be evaluated based on their potential return after accounting for taxes, ensuring that they contribute positively to your overall financial health.

7. Avoiding Overcommitment: Properly accounting for taxes helps prevent overcommitment of funds that might be needed to meet tax obligations. For instance, relying on VAT refunds as a source of immediate cash flow can be risky, as it overlooks the fact that VAT is a liability that will need to be settled.

8. Timely Tax Preparation: Understanding the impact of taxes on profitability enables you to plan for and prepare taxes in a timely manner. This is especially important for taxes like corporate tax, which may have a delayed payment deadline. Being prepared and setting aside funds in advance can prevent last-minute financial strain.

In summary, understanding profitability by accurately accounting for taxes is crucial for making sound financial decisions, ensuring long-term sustainability, and maintaining compliance with tax obligations. By removing VAT, corporate tax, and employment taxes from your financial analysis, you can gain a more realistic and actionable perspective on your business's financial performance.

Understanding Cash Accounting & Accrual Accounting

Cash Accounting & Accrual Accounting: Cash accounting is an accounting method that focuses on recording transactions when cash is exchanged. This means that revenue and expenses are only recognised when money changes hands, rather than when invoices are sent or received.

Accounting

Cash accounting is often used by small businesses, as it simplifies record keeping and can provide a more accurate picture of a business's short-term financial health. However, it can also lead to issues if not managed carefully, such as delayed recognition of income and problems matching expenses to the correct period.

Accrual accounting is a method of accounting that focuses on recording transactions when they occur, regardless of when cash is exchanged. This means that revenue and expenses are recognised when invoices are sent or received, rather than when money changes hands. Accrual accounting is the most common type of accounting used by businesses, as it provides a more accurate picture of a business's financial health over time.

However, it can be more complex than cash accounting and may require more detailed record-keeping. If you're thinking of using accrual accounting for your business, it's important to speak to an accountant or tax advisor first to make sure it's the right decision for you.

Accounting

Monthly Reviews

Reviewing the profit and loss (P&L) statement of a business on a monthly basis is crucial for several reasons:

Performance Assessment: Assess your business's financial health and performance by tracking revenue, expenses, and profitability over time. Spot trends, positive or negative.

Swift Decision-Making: Regular P&L analysis supports quick decisions. Identify profit drops or expense spikes and take immediate action to adjust strategies.

Budget Alignment: Compare actual results with budget projections to stay on financial track. Adjust spending and revenue tactics for consistency.

Cash Flow Insight: P&L reviews reveal cash flow patterns. Forecast low periods and manage working capital effectively.

Consistent Performance Yardstick: Gauge performance trends over time for insights into seasonal fluctuations or deviations requiring attention.

Accounting

Spotting Growth Avenues: Identify growth opportunities by analysing strong revenue sources and new markets to explore. Adapt strategies accordingly.

Building Stakeholder Trust: Provide investors, lenders, and stakeholders with transparent P&L statements to maintain confidence and trust.

Strategic Decision-Making: Detailed financial insights empower smart choices about investments, expansions, and resource allocation.

Monthly tax management is a practice in financial management with far-reaching benefits:

Stay Current: Regular tax oversight keeps you in sync with deadlines, avoiding last-minute rushes.

Prevent Overload: Consistent attention prevents taxes from piling up and straining your finances.

Smart Cash Flow: Manage taxes monthly for smoother cash flow planning, ensuring stability amidst expenses.

Transparent Finances: Regular tax tracking maintains transparent financial records, vital for stakeholder trust.

Tax Optimisation: Monthly reviews reveal tax-saving opportunities that could otherwise be missed.

Proactive Strategy: Engage in legal tax reduction strategies, enhancing financial efficiency. Ongoing management eases year-end tax preparations, alleviating stress.

Monthly Monitoring of Liabilities: Maintaining Financial Health

Short-Term Liabilities:

Monthly reviews of short-term responsibilities are essential for smooth business operations.

Resource Allocation: Assessments guide effective resource allocation, prioritising payments and addressing pressing concerns.

Creditor Relations: Monitoring fosters positive relations with creditors through timely payments and proactive communication.

Budget Precision: Insights lead to accurate budget adjustments, avoiding short-term liability mismatches.

Informed Decisions: Knowing liabilities shapes informed choices about investments and resource distribution. Monitoring prevents overcommitment, safeguarding against financial strain and defaults.

Accounting

Long-Term Liabilities:

Monthly review of long-term liabilities brings advantages:

Strategic Alignment: Regular reviews sync strategies with obligations, ensuring feasibility and sustainability.

Risk Anticipation: Consistent checks identify long-term risk possibilities, guiding mitigation strategies.

Resource Efficiency: Monthly review allocates resources for long-term obligations without disrupting operations.

Cash Flow Projection: Monitoring predicts cash needs, facilitating planning and financing for obligations.

Budget Precision: Insights guide budget adjustments, enabling a balance between commitments and resources.

Informed Investments: Awareness shapes investment decisions, evaluating capacity for growth without overextension.

Compliance and Reputation: Regular reviews ensure obligation compliance and positive reputation.

Accounting

Quarterly Reviews

Regular quarterly reviews of profitability trends deliver essential benefits:

Performance Snapshot: Shorter time frames reveal fluctuations and patterns, driving informed responses. Early spotting of declining profits enables proactive correction. Detect potential growth areas by identifying high-profit contributors.

Decision Foundation: Timely data informs resource allocation, investments, and strategies.

Adaptation Agility: Respond to market shifts promptly for effective adjustments.

Stakeholder Assurance: Investors value transparent, quarterly profitability updates.

Long-Term Direction: Trends guide future plans, ensuring continuity.

Quarterly assessment of long-term liabilities is pivotal:

Trend Insight: Spot emerging problems or opportunities, enabling timely actions.

Enhanced Planning: Refine financial plans, manage cash flow, and set goals.

Resource Wisdom: Allocate capital for long-term obligations wisely.

Stakeholder Trust: Demonstrates transparency, boosting confidence.

Innovation Culture: Foster solutions for efficient liability management.

Regular product pipeline assessments offer numerous advantages:

Strategic Alignment: Ensures new products match overall business goals.

Resource Efficiency: Efficient allocation of resources for optimal results.

Risk Mitigation: Identifies risks and prevents delays or failures.

Market Relevance: Keeps products aligned with evolving market needs.

Competitive Edge: Prioritise unique value propositions for market dominance.

Customer Engagement: Integrates customer feedback for successful development.

Efficiency Boost: Streamlines product development, reducing time-to-market.

Performance Evaluation: Measures progress against goals for data-driven adjustments.

Accounting

Confirming IP & Domain Ownership:

> Verify the ownership status of intellectual property assets to protect the business's creative work and innovations. Confirm registrations, licenses, and agreements to prevent legal complications and ensure proper rights management. This safeguards against unauthorised use and preserves the IP integrity.

> Domain management reviews include a thorough check on the ownership and renewal status of primary domains. This safeguards against domain hijacking attempts and maintains uninterrupted access to the company's digital resources. Consider purchasing similar domain names that could potentially be used by competitors or malicious entities to mislead customers or infringe on your brand.

Annual Investment Allowance

The UK Annual Investment Allowance (AIA) is a tax incentive provided by the government to encourage businesses to invest in qualifying capital assets. It allows businesses to deduct the full value of eligible capital expenditures from their taxable profits in the year of purchase, up to a certain limit. This deduction can significantly reduce a business's tax liability, providing a financial incentive for companies to invest in assets that support growth, innovation, and environmental sustainability.

Accounting

The AIA limit is £1 million per year. This means that businesses can deduct up to £1 million of qualifying capital expenditures from their taxable profits, effectively reducing the amount of tax they owe. The AIA can apply to a wide range of capital assets, and it has the potential to provide a substantial tax benefit for businesses that make significant investments.

Here are some key points to understand about the UK Annual Investment Allowance and its implications for businesses:

1. Eligible Assets: The AIA can be used for a variety of assets, including but not limited to:

- Electric cars and vehicles with zero CO2 emissions.
- Plant and machinery for gas refuelling stations, such as storage tanks and pumps for gas, biogas, and hydrogen refuelling.
- Zero-emission goods vehicles.
- Equipment for electric vehicle charging points.
- Most other plant and machinery used for business purposes.

2. Timing of Deduction: The AIA allows businesses to claim the full value of qualifying capital expenditures as a deduction in the year of purchase. This is in contrast to other forms of capital allowances, which typically involve spreading the deduction over several years.

3. Annual Limit: The AIA limit sets the maximum amount that can be deducted in a single tax year. As of your last update, the limit is £1 million per year. However, it's important to note that this limit can change, so businesses should stay updated on any revisions to the AIA threshold.

4. Impact on Tax Liability: By deducting the cost of eligible assets from their taxable profits, businesses can significantly reduce their tax liability for the year. This can free up funds that can be reinvested in the business for further growth, expansion, or innovation.

5. Encouragement of Sustainable Practices: The AIA's inclusion of assets related to environmental sustainability, such as electric vehicles and charging equipment, aligns with the government's goals to promote eco-friendly practices and reduce carbon emissions.

6. Planning and Strategy: Businesses can strategically plan their capital expenditures to maximise the benefits of the AIA. For example, if a business is considering purchasing qualifying assets, it may be advantageous to time the purchases to optimise the use of the AIA within the annual limit.

7. Consultation with Tax Professionals: Navigating the complexities of tax incentives like the AIA may require the expertise of tax professionals. Consulting with tax advisors or accountants can help businesses ensure that they fully understand the rules and implications of utilising the AIA.

In conclusion, the UK Annual Investment Allowance is a valuable tool that can provide substantial tax savings for businesses investing in qualifying capital assets. It incentivises companies to make strategic investments in equipment, vehicles, and technologies that can drive growth, improve efficiency, and support environmental sustainability. Businesses should carefully consider how they can leverage the AIA to optimise their tax position and make informed investment decisions.

Business Asset Disposal Relief

Business Asset Disposal Relief is a tax relief scheme in the United Kingdom that allows individuals to reduce the amount of Capital Gains Tax (CGT) they pay when disposing of certain business assets. The relief aims to incentivise entrepreneurship and reward individuals who have built and operated successful businesses.

As of 2023, Business Asset Disposal Relief allows eligible individuals to pay a reduced rate of 10% on qualifying gains, up to a lifetime limit of £1,000,000. This means that if you sell part or all of your business and make a capital gain, you'll only be liable to pay 10% tax on that gain, up to the specified lifetime limit.

This is a significantly lower rate compared to the standard Capital Gains Tax rate, which can be as high as 20% or 28%, depending on your total income and the nature of the gain.

Here are some key points to understand about Business Asset Disposal Relief:

Eligibility Criteria: To qualify for the relief, you typically need to meet certain conditions, including being an individual or a partner in a business, holding at least 5% of the shares and voting rights in a company, and being involved in the business's management for a specified period. These criteria may vary and change over time, so it's essential to consult with a qualified financial or legal advisor to ensure your eligibility.

Qualifying Assets: The relief applies to the disposal of certain business assets, including shares, land, and business assets used in your trade. It's important to note that not all types of assets are eligible for the relief, so understanding which assets qualify is crucial.

Lifetime Limit: There is a lifetime limit on the total amount of gains that can benefit from the relief. As of 2023, this limit is £1,000,000. Any qualifying gains made beyond this limit would be subject to the standard Capital Gains Tax rates.

Changes Over the Years: The lifetime limit and other aspects of the relief have changed over the years due to updates in tax legislation.

Accounting

It's advisable to stay informed about any changes and seek professional advice to ensure you're taking advantage of the most up-to-date information.

Consulting Professionals: Given the complexity of tax law and the specific eligibility criteria, it's highly recommended to work closely with a qualified accountant, financial, or legal advisor before making any decisions related to Business Asset Disposal Relief. Attempting to navigate this process without professional guidance could lead to mistakes or missed opportunities.

In summary, Business Asset Disposal Relief is a tax relief scheme in the UK designed to encourage entrepreneurship and provide tax benefits to individuals who sell part or all of their qualifying business assets. However, due to the evolving nature of tax regulations and the complexity of eligibility criteria, seeking expert advice is essential to ensure you fully understand your eligibility and the potential tax implications of your business asset disposal.

Investor Relief

Investor's Relief is a tax relief scheme in the United Kingdom that provides certain investors with a reduced rate of Capital Gains Tax (CGT) when they sell qualifying shares. The relief is designed to encourage investment in businesses and startups, particularly by individuals who provide capital but do not play an active role in the business's management.

132

Accounting

Key points to understand about Investor's Relief include:

Holding Period: To qualify for Investor's Relief, you must have held the shares for a continuous period of at least 3 years before the sale. This requirement ensures that the relief benefits long-term investors who have a genuine interest in the company's success.

Connection to the Business: Unlike some other tax reliefs, you cannot be connected to the business in certain ways. This means you cannot have a relative or friend who is working for the business. The goal is to ensure that the relief is targeted at passive investors rather than those actively involved in the company's operations.

Lifetime Limit: There is a lifetime limit on the total amount of gains that can benefit from Investor's Relief, £10 million. This means that you can only claim the reduced rate of CGT on gains up to this limit.

Type of Shares: To be eligible for Investor's Relief, you must hold ordinary, fully paid-up shares in the company. This means that preference shares or other types of shares may not qualify for the relief.

Trading Company or Group: The company in which you hold the shares must be a trading company or the holding company of a trading group. This requirement ensures that the relief supports businesses engaged in trading activities rather than non-trading or investment activities.

Accounting

Employee Status: Neither you nor any person connected to you can be an employee of the company or a company connected to it. This is to prevent individuals who are actively involved in the business from benefiting from the relief.

Stock Exchange Listing: None of the shares for which you are claiming Investor's Relief can be listed or traded on a recognised stock exchange.

Reduced Capital Gains Tax: If you meet all the qualifying criteria, you would be required to pay a reduced rate of 10% Capital Gains Tax on the qualifying gains from the sale of the shares. This is significantly lower than the standard rates of CGT.

Professional Advice: Given the complexity of the eligibility criteria and the potential tax implications, it's crucial to consult with a qualified legal advisor before attempting to claim Investor's Relief. Professional guidance is essential to ensure that you meet all the requirements and take full advantage of the relief.

In summary, Investor's Relief provides an opportunity for passive investors to benefit from a reduced rate of Capital Gains Tax when selling qualifying shares in a trading company or group.

Accounting

Capital Gains Tax vs. Income Tax

Capital Gains Tax (CGT) and Income Tax are both taxes imposed by the UK government, but they apply to different types of financial transactions and income sources. Here's a comparison between the two:

Capital Gains Tax:

CGT is a tax on the profit made when you sell or dispose of an asset that has increased in value.

It applies to a wide range of assets, including property, investments, and personal belongings, subject to certain exemptions and reliefs.

The current standard CGT rates in the UK are 10% for basic rate taxpayers and 20% for higher and additional rate taxpayers. The rates may vary depending on the type of asset and your overall income.

The annual exempt amount (known as the "tax-free allowance") allows you to make a certain amount of gains each tax year without incurring CGT. The annual exempt amount is around £12,300 for individuals (subject to change).

Income Tax:

Income Tax is a tax on various types of income, such as wages, salaries, rental income, dividends, and interest.

It applies to your total income from all sources, including employment, self-employment, pensions, and savings.

Income Tax rates are progressive, meaning they increase as your income rises. Basic rate, higher rate, and additional rate taxpayers pay different rates.

The current rates and thresholds for Income Tax may change annually and depend on your personal circumstances.

Capital Gains Tax vs. Income Tax Considerations:

Choosing whether to sell assets to realise capital gains or receive income through other means involves various factors, including your overall financial goals, tax planning, and potential investment risks.

The choice between realising capital gains and receiving income can impact your effective tax rate and overall tax liability.

Tax planning should consider both CGT and Income Tax implications to optimise your financial situation.

Importance of VAT Registration:

Value Added Tax (VAT) is a consumption tax applied to the value added at each stage of the supply chain for goods and services. VAT is collected by businesses on behalf of the government and is paid by the end consumer.

Accounting

VAT-registered businesses charge VAT on their sales (output tax) and reclaim VAT on their purchases (input tax), and the difference is remitted to the tax authorities.

Key Points about VAT Registration:

Thresholds: Businesses must register for VAT if their taxable turnover exceeds the VAT registration threshold. The threshold is £85,000. However, it's important to note that thresholds and rules may change over time.

Voluntary Registration: Even if your turnover is below the threshold, you can choose to register for VAT voluntarily. This might be advantageous if you want to reclaim VAT on your business expenses or if being VAT-registered benefits your business relationships.

Benefits of VAT Registration: VAT registration allows businesses to reclaim input tax, enhancing cash flow. It also enables your business to appear more established and credible, as VAT registration is often seen as a sign of a larger or more established company.

Compliance Requirements: VAT registration comes with compliance obligations, including accurate record-keeping, submitting VAT returns on time, and charging the correct rate of VAT on sales.

Penalties: Failing to register for VAT when required can result in penalties and backdated VAT liability.

Accounting

In conclusion, understanding the differences between Capital Gains Tax and Income Tax is essential for effective tax planning. VAT registration is crucial for businesses that meet the relevant thresholds to comply with tax regulations and manage their financial operations efficiently.

VAT Exemptions

Recognising VAT exemptions and understanding the right methods of delivery is crucial for businesses operating in the UK to ensure compliance with tax regulations and manage their financial operations effectively. Value Added Tax (VAT) is a consumption tax that is levied on the value added to goods and services at each stage of production or distribution. It's an important source of revenue for governments and helps fund public services.

Importance of Recognising VAT Exemptions:

Compliance with Tax Regulations: Accurately identifying and applying VAT exemptions ensures that a business complies with UK tax laws. Failing to do so could result in penalties, fines, or legal consequences.

Financial Management: Recognising VAT exemptions helps businesses manage their finances more effectively. By correctly categorising products and services, businesses can accurately calculate their tax liabilities, which in turn influences pricing strategies, profit margins, and overall financial planning.

Accounting

Competitive Advantage: Correctly applying VAT exemptions can provide a competitive advantage. If a business can offer certain products or services as VAT-exempt, it may attract more customers or clients who are sensitive to pricing.

Cost Efficiency: Understanding VAT exemptions can help businesses optimise their supply chains and procurement processes. If certain items are VAT-exempt, businesses can better plan their purchasing and avoid unnecessary tax costs.

Customer Trust: Transparently applying VAT exemptions and accurately representing prices can build trust with customers, who may appreciate the upfront and honest approach.

Methods of Delivery and VAT Rates:

The method of delivery can significantly impact the VAT rate applied to a product or service. The UK's VAT rules differentiate between physical and digital products, as well as different methods of delivery. Here are a few examples:

Electronic Books: Electronic books (e-books) are considered digital services. In the UK, e-books are subject to a zero VAT rate. This means that no VAT is charged on the sale of e-books, making them more affordable for consumers.

Accounting

Website Subscription Services: If a business provides access to content or services through a subscription-based website, the VAT rate may differ based on the nature of the content. Some types of content might be subject to the standard VAT rate (currently 20%), while others could potentially qualify for reduced rates or exemptions.

Physical Goods: The VAT rate on physical goods can vary depending on the type of product. For example, most basic food items, children's clothing, and books are subject to a reduced rate of 5% VAT, while other goods are subject to the standard rate of 20%.

Distance Selling: When selling goods to customers in other EU countries (prior to the UK's exit from the EU), different VAT rules applied based on the value of the goods and the destination country. These rules aimed to ensure fair competition and compliance with VAT regulations across borders.

It's important for businesses to accurately determine the VAT treatment of their products and services based on the method of delivery, product type, and relevant regulations.

Consulting with tax professionals or using accounting software that specialises in VAT calculations can help ensure accurate compliance.

Businesses that accurately apply VAT rules can benefit from improved financial planning, competitive advantages, and stronger customer relationships.

Accounting

Business Rates

Business rates, also known as non-domestic rates, are a form of local taxation in the United Kingdom that businesses must pay on their commercial properties. These rates contribute to funding local services provided by local authorities, such as schools, roads, waste collection, and other essential services. The rates are calculated based on the rental value of the property and are typically revalued every five years to reflect changes in property values.

Business rates are a significant cost for many businesses, and as such, various methods of reduction have been implemented to support businesses and encourage economic growth. Some of the methods of reducing business rates in the UK include:

Small Business Rate Relief (SBRR): This relief is aimed at supporting small businesses with relatively low property values. If the rateable value of a property is below a certain threshold (usually £15,000 or £12,000 in London), the business may be eligible for a reduction in their business rates.

In some cases, businesses with properties with a rateable value of up to £50,000 may receive partial relief.

Rural Rate Relief: Businesses in rural areas may qualify for this relief if their property is in a designated rural settlement with a population of less than 3,000.

The level of relief depends on the population of the settlement.

Charitable Rate Relief: Charities and registered community amateur sports clubs can apply for this relief, which provides a reduction of up to 80% on the business rates for properties used for charitable purposes.

Enterprise Zones: Enterprise zones are designated areas where businesses can receive various incentives, including business rate discounts and enhanced capital allowances for investments in plant and machinery. These zones are meant to encourage economic development and job creation.

Empty Property Relief: Properties that are unoccupied for a certain period may qualify for empty property relief. While the exact rules and duration of relief vary by location, this relief can provide temporary relief from business rates for vacant properties.

Retail Discount: In certain years, the UK government has introduced retail discounts to support retail businesses.

These discounts, often introduced as temporary measures, provide a percentage reduction in business rates for eligible retail properties.

Hardship Relief: Local authorities have the discretion to grant hardship relief to businesses facing financial difficulties. This relief is typically granted on a case-by-case basis.

Accounting

Transitional Relief: To ease the impact of significant changes in property values after a revaluation, transitional relief is provided. This gradually phases in increases or decreases in business rates over a set period.

It's important to note that the specific details and availability of these relief measures may change over time, as they are subject to government policy and local authority decisions. Businesses interested in reducing their business rates should consult with their local council or relevant authorities to understand the eligibility criteria and application process for these relief measures.

Dividend vs Income (Salary)

"Dividend" and "income" (specifically referring to salary) are both terms related to how individuals earn money from their investments or employment, respectively. A dividend is a payment made by a corporation to its shareholders as a distribution of profits.

It's a portion of the company's earnings that is returned to the owners of the company's stock. Dividends are typically paid out on a regular basis, such as quarterly or annually, and are usually expressed as a certain amount per share. Here are some key points about dividends:

Source: Dividends come from a company's net profits. After covering expenses and reinvestment needs, a company's board of directors may decide to distribute a portion of the profits to shareholders.

Accounting

Tax Treatment: In many countries, including the United Kingdom, dividends are subject to a different tax treatment compared to other forms of income. They are often taxed at a lower rate known as the "dividend tax rate."

Investor Ownership: Dividends are typically distributed to shareholders in proportion to their ownership of the company. If you own more shares, you receive a larger portion of the dividend payout.

Volatility: Dividend payments can vary based on the company's financial performance and management's decisions. Companies may increase, decrease, or even suspend dividend payments based on their circumstances.

Income, in the context of salary, refers to the compensation an individual receives for providing services or work as an employee of a company or organisation. This is often in the form of a regular paycheck and can include other benefits such as health insurance, retirement contributions, and bonuses. Here are some key points about salary income:

Source: Income is earned by providing labour, skills, or services to a business. It is a direct result of the work performed.

Tax Treatment: Salary income is typically subject to regular income tax rates. The tax amount is usually withheld by the business and paid to the government on behalf of the employee.

Accounting

Predictability: Salary income is generally more predictable and stable than dividends. Employees receive a regular paycheck based on their employment contract.

Employment Relationship: Income is earned through an employment relationship, where an individual works for a company and follows its rules and policies.

The choice between dividends and salary income depends on an individual's financial goals, circumstances, and investment preferences. Some investors prioritise dividends for passive income and potential tax advantages, while others seek salary income for its stability and consistency.

For business owners, the decision between dividends and salary income involves careful consideration of various factors, including the nature of the business, tax implications, and personal financial goals. Business owners who are also shareholders have the unique opportunity to influence how they receive compensation.

Dividends can provide a tax-efficient way to access profits, especially in jurisdictions where dividend tax rates are lower than regular income tax rates. Owners can strategically time dividend distributions to align with their financial needs and optimise their tax liabilities.

Accounting

On the other hand, salary income offers consistency and can help business owners establish a stable personal income stream, which can be particularly important during the early stages of a business when profits may be reinvested. Additionally, salary income may enhance eligibility for certain benefits, such as social security contributions, pension plans, and loans, which can contribute to long-term financial security.

Ultimately, the choice between dividends and salary income for business owners depends on a holistic evaluation of financial objectives, business strategy, and the desire for a balance between immediate income and long-term stability. Seeking advice from financial experts and tax professionals is crucial to making an informed decision tailored to the owner's specific circumstances.

An example of how a mix of dividends and salary can work for a business owner and what it entails.

Example:

Imagine you are the owner of a small consulting firm that provides specialised IT services to clients. You own 100% of the company's shares.

As the owner, you have the flexibility to determine how you receive compensation from the business. You have two main options: taking a combination of dividends and salary.

Accounting

Dividends: Let's say your company had a profitable year, generating £100,000 in net profits after deducting all expenses, taxes, and reinvestment needs. You decide to distribute £40,000 of these profits as dividends to yourself as the shareholder. This dividend distribution is proportionate to your ownership of the company, which is 100%.

Salary: In addition to dividends, you decide to pay yourself a salary of £60,000 for your role as the CEO and lead consultant of the firm. This salary reflects the value of your work and expertise in driving the company's success.

What It Means: This mix of dividends and salary provides you with a balanced approach to compensation as a business owner.

Dividends: By receiving dividends, you are able to access a portion of the company's profits directly. Dividends are typically subject to a lower tax rate than regular income, making this an efficient way to take money out of the business. The £40,000 in dividends contributes to your personal income and financial goals.

Salary: The £60,000 salary provides you with a stable and consistent income stream. This can be particularly beneficial for covering your personal expenses and maintaining a steady standard of living. The salary also helps you establish a reliable income to support your financial commitments.

Financial Flexibility: The combination of dividends and salary offers financial flexibility. Dividends allow you to benefit directly from the company's success, while the salary ensures you have a dependable income, especially during periods of business fluctuations or lower profits.

Tax Considerations: Dividends and salary are taxed differently. Dividends may be subject to lower dividend tax rates, while the salary is subject to regular income tax rates. The specific tax implications will depend on the tax laws in your jurisdiction.

Long-Term Planning: This approach supports both short-term financial needs and long-term planning. Dividends can contribute to your immediate income, while the salary helps you build a stable financial foundation for retirement, investments, and other long-term goals.

Owner's Perspective: The decision to balance dividends and salary reflects your understanding of the business's financial health, your personal financial goals, and your desire to optimise your compensation structure for both immediate and future benefits.

Remember that the mix of dividends and salary should be determined based on various factors, including the company's financial performance, tax implications, legal requirements, and your personal financial objectives. Consulting with financial advisors and tax professionals is essential to make informed decisions tailored to your unique situation.

Accounting

Crashes

Case Study: Learning from the Collapse of a Café Chain

The collapse of a once-thriving UK café chain offers a stark lesson on the vital role owners and management play in steering a company's finances. It underscores the importance of owners grasping their company's financial health and controls. When owners delegate without staying involved, it can lead to serious consequences.

This case vividly shows the aftermath of poor financial management and how it can affect a company. An investigation by the Financial Reporting Council (FRC) found failures in financial management, audits, and governance.

Despite being a major UK chain with many cafes and a large workforce, the downfall was due to a serious lack of financial understanding at the top levels. The owner lacked a serious understanding of financial controls. This lack of oversight extended to other top executives, including the finance director.

The finance director failed to catch fraudulent activities. They were later arrested for fraud and forgery. This exposed a web of financial deceit including fake invoices and payments. This caused the company accounts to be overstated by a huge £94 million.

Accounting

The company's auditing firm also failed to properly check the company's finances. They missed warning signs and accepted the company's figures without proper review.

After the collapse, there were significant job losses and damage to the both the café and the auditing firms reputation. The effects went beyond finances, shaking the trust of stakeholders, customers, and investors.

This case study teaches us the importance of owners being actively involved in understanding and managing finances. It shows that having strong financial controls, impartial audits, and a transparent culture in a company is crucial. Delegating financial oversight can lead to serious problems, as seen in this café chain's downfall.

Staff to Revenue Ratio

The staff-to-revenue ratio is a vital metric used by businesses to gauge the efficiency of their workforce in generating revenue. It reflects the relationship between a company's revenue and the number of full-time equivalent (FTE) staff it employs.

This ratio serves as a valuable tool for measuring productivity, assessing business performance, and making informed decisions about resource allocation and growth strategies.

Accounting

For instance, if a business generates £1 million in revenue and has 10 full-time equivalent staff members, the staff-to-revenue ratio would be £100,000 per employee. This ratio can vary widely across different industries and sectors, with factors like labour intensity, business model, and technology adoption influencing the ideal ratio.

The staff-to-revenue ratio holds particular significance in guiding productivity and growth objectives. By setting a target or benchmark for this ratio, businesses can strive to achieve optimal efficiency. However, a careful balance is necessary. On one hand, maintaining a low ratio can indicate high productivity, where a relatively small workforce generates substantial revenue. On the other hand, an extremely low ratio might signal an overworked staff or resource constraints, potentially compromising the quality of products or services.

Conversely, an excessively high ratio could indicate inefficient resource allocation, where an excessive number of employees are generating inadequate revenue. This scenario often leads to reduced profit margins and impedes the scalability of the business.

Unfortunately, the UK business landscape has encountered challenges related to adding more staff without a corresponding increase in revenue, leading to decreased profitability.

Accounting

Effectively managing the staff-to-revenue ratio requires a strategic approach. As a business grows, it's essential to ensure that revenue growth outpaces the expansion of the workforce. This can involve leveraging technology and process improvements to enhance productivity, evaluating the necessity of each new hire, and continuously monitoring and adjusting the ratio to align with industry norms and the company's goals.

The staff-to-revenue ratio's value lies not only in its ability to assess productivity but also in its role as a key performance indicator (KPI) that informs decision-making. By focusing on optimising this ratio, businesses can enhance efficiency, allocate resources more effectively, and drive sustainable growth while maintaining healthy profit margins. In summary, while business growth is a crucial objective, it's equally essential to ensure that the increase in staff aligns harmoniously with revenue growth to maintain a competitive and profitable business model.

Implementing the following strategies and documents can aid in managing the staff-to-revenue ratio effectively, ensuring that your business maintains a healthy balance between workforce size and revenue generation:

Monitoring Profit/Loss: Regularly tracking your business's profit and loss (P&L) statements provides insights into your financial performance. By analysing revenue trends, costs, and expenses, you can identify patterns that impact your staff-to-revenue ratio.

If the ratio starts to skew unfavourably, adjustments can be made proactively to align staffing levels with revenue growth.

Management of Accounts: Thoroughly managing your accounts involves monitoring receivables, payables, and cash flow. Timely collection of payments and efficient payments of expenses directly impacts your revenue. Effective accounts management can ensure a steady cash flow, which in turn supports the sustainability of your staff-to-revenue ratio.

FINKPI (Financial Key Performance Indicators): Select and focus on key financial KPIs that directly influence your staff-to-revenue ratio. Examples include Gross Profit Margin, Net Profit Margin, Revenue Growth Rate, and Cost of Goods Sold (COGS) as a percentage of revenue. Regularly measuring and analysing these KPIs allows you to make informed decisions to maintain a healthy ratio.

Conduct Strategy Reviews with Action Items: Periodically review your business strategy using the A3 strategy document to assess its alignment with the staff-to-revenue ratio goals. If discrepancies are identified, develop actionable steps to address them.

This might involve optimising processes, reallocating resources, or exploring new revenue streams. Strategy reviews ensure that your business remains adaptable and responsive to changes in the ratio.

Develop People with a Creative Management Team: Your management team plays a crucial role in optimising the staff-to-revenue ratio. Encourage creative thinking and problem-solving among your managers. Empower them to identify opportunities for streamlining operations, maximising employee productivity, and fostering a culture of innovation. Engaged and motivated employees can contribute to higher revenue generation without excessive workforce growth.

By implementing these strategies and documents, you can create a comprehensive approach to managing the staff-to-revenue ratio.

Awareness of the Director's Liability

Directors are overall responsible for the management of a business's operations; they make strategic decisions and help the company and their team grow. With such a duty of care, often comes personal liability.

As a director, you can be held personally liable for many legal issues, but why and when would this happen?

Director's Guarantees are one of the easiest ways owners of a company royally screw themselves over. The guarantee usually comes into play when taking out bank loans for a company.

Accounting

The director personally commits by signing a contract to repay the debt if the business is unable to meet the obligation, due to either financial troubles in which payments must fall elsewhere (such as payroll) or bankruptcy.

For example, in terms of a commercial property lease with a director's guarantee, the director of a company signs a contract to say that they personally guarantee the payment of rent.

This means that if there's an absence of company finances and the business fails to meet its obligations under the lease, the director is personally responsible for fulfilling those obligations. The landlord can demand payment from the director who signed the director's guarantee.

The director's guarantee serves as an assurance to the landlord that the lease obligations will be met, even if the business is unable to do so.

SME directors are the usual victims of director guarantees, directors of larger companies that turn over millions are less likely to be asked for one.

The issue with a director's guarantee is that many SME owners don't know what it is they're signing or getting themselves into.

This is not because they're irresponsible but because they don't know what they haven't been taught, and many entrepreneurs aren't taught about these legally binding documents.

By signing a director guarantee, the responsibility legally falls on the director personally and they will be pursued for the money with little negotiation from the lending party. By not signing one, if financial trouble did occur, there's more room for negotiation with the lending party.

It can be difficult to borrow money, open trading accounts with suppliers, or lease a property as an SME, as there's little capital for the lenders to go off which shows the cash flow in a business is reliable. That's why they ask directors of SMEs to sign a guarantee.

The BAMTM recommendation is to seek legal advice before signing a guarantee of any kind. Advice of this kind will need to be taken through a third party and not the bank or lender themselves.

A solicitor would be the best bet in this situation, as they will be able to break down the document and get to know the business situation. Through this understanding, the solicitor will be able to advise you to the best of their ability.

Accounting

Too Much Money Available to Companies

A common phenomenon in business management and decision-making is that many business owners do not feel the need to take proactive measures to optimise their workforce and operations when they have significant cash reserves.

Complacency and Overconfidence: Human beings are inherently optimistic creatures. When a business is enjoying high profits and has ample cash reserves, there can be a tendency towards complacency and overconfidence. Decision-makers might believe that the good times will continue indefinitely, leading them to delay making tough decisions about cost optimisation, including staffing levels.

Fear of Alienating Employees and Impact on Morale: Removing unproductive or problematic team members, especially during prosperous times, can lead to fear of alienating loyal teams and damaging overall morale.

Lack of Urgency: Having a significant amount of cash on hand can create a sense of security and reduce the perceived urgency to make immediate changes. When a recession hits and cash flow becomes tight, the pressure to make difficult decisions intensifies.

Short-Term vs. Long-Term Focus: Businesses might prioritise short-term gains and focus on capitalising on the immediate opportunities presented during periods of economic prosperity.

They may not allocate sufficient attention to longer-term strategies, including workforce optimisation and contingency planning, until a crisis necessitates it.

The Uncertainty of Economic Forecasting: Predicting economic downturns with precision is challenging. Businesses might be aware of potential risks, but the exact timing and severity of a recession are difficult to predict. This uncertainty can lead to a lack of proactive action.

In summary, the behaviour of businesses in not making hard decisions until a recession hits is influenced by a combination of psychological, cultural, economic, and organisational factors. The nature of decision-making often involves a delicate balance between short-term gains, long-term stability, emotional considerations, and the uncertainty of future economic conditions. Recognising these influences and striving for a balance between proactive decision-making and prudent financial management is crucial for businesses aiming to navigate economic cycles successfully.

Family Members That Work Within the Business

A common strategy employed by numerous businesses involves engaging family members, such as children, spouses, or husbands and wives, to contribute to the operations of the enterprise.

This approach allows for the optimisation of the complete salary allocation, ensuring that the available tax allowances are fully utilised.

It's worth noting that this tactic necessitates active involvement in the business on the part of the family member. Merely designating someone as an employee isn't sufficient; they should genuinely participate in the business's activities. By doing so, the business can appropriately leverage the tax-free allowance while adhering to the stipulated regulations and maintaining ethical practices.

Capitalising on this arrangement can offer a dual benefit: it enables the business to take advantage of tax-efficient compensation distribution, while concurrently assisting family members, particularly children, in amassing the financial resources required for venturing into the property market. However, it's imperative to ensure that all actions are conducted in accordance with legal and regulatory frameworks, underscoring the genuine involvement of family members in the business operations to warrant the utilisation of tax allowances.

Share Options for Key Personnel

Share options for key personnel refers to a compensation and incentive strategy employed by businesses, where certain employees are granted the right to purchase shares of the company's stock at a predetermined price within a specified time frame.

This approach is often used to attract, retain, and motivate key employees by offering them a potential stake in the company's future growth and success.

Accounting

Here are some important aspects to consider when discussing share options for employees:

Employee Stock Options (ESOs): Employee stock options are contractual agreements that allow employees to purchase a specific number of company shares (stock options) at a set price during a predetermined period, usually referred to as the vesting period. The idea is that if the company's stock price increases over time, employees can exercise their options and purchase shares at a lower price, potentially realising a profit.

Vesting Period: The vesting period is the time frame over which an employee needs to stay with the company before they can exercise their stock options. Vesting is designed to encourage employee loyalty and commitment. Once the options are vested, the employee can exercise them and buy shares.

Exercise Price: The exercise price is the predetermined price at which employees can buy the company's stock when they exercise their options. It's often set at the current market price at the time the options are granted or at a discount to that price.

Potential Benefits:

Employee Incentives: Share options align the interests of employees with those of shareholders, as employees benefit from the company's success.

Retention Tool: Offering share options can help retain key personnel, as they have an incentive to remain with the company to fully realise the potential gains from the options.

Motivation and Performance: Employees may be motivated to contribute to the company's growth and profitability to increase the value of their potential future shares.

Talent Attraction: Share options can be an attractive component of compensation packages, helping companies attract top talent.

Tax Implications: Tax treatment of employee stock options can vary depending on the jurisdiction and specific plan structure. In some cases, there may be tax advantages to certain types of stock option plans. It's crucial for both the company and employees to understand the tax implications.

Risks and Considerations:

Stock Price Volatility: The value of the options is tied to the company's stock price, which can be volatile. Employees may not realise any value if the stock price doesn't increase.

Liquidity: Employees need to have the funds available to exercise their options and purchase shares.

Dilution: Issuing additional shares through stock option plans can dilute the ownership stakes of existing shareholders.

Communication and Transparency: Clear communication about the terms, potential benefits, and risks of the stock option plan is essential to ensure employees understand what they are being offered.

Overall, share options for key personnel can be a valuable tool for companies to reward and incentivise their employees, aligning their interests with the company's growth. However, designing an effective and fair share option plan requires careful consideration of legal, financial, and strategic factors, and consulting with legal, financial, and tax professionals is highly recommended.

Management

Management

The Differences in Management

Strategic Managers are the management team or directors that decide the strategy and approach for the company for the next 12 months, 24 months, or 5 years. The strategy is decided by the strategic managers but there is input from the operation managers.

Strategic managers will also take responsibility for the long-term financial management of a company.

Their role is to think long-term and look forward as a business, to ensure that there is not only money in place for developing projects but that the projects they have planned align with the aims of the business.

Operation Managers are the management team that develop and oversee the company teams daily. They determine the processes to be implemented within the business that help operations run efficiently and understand what activities or tasks are feasible.

Operation management is a very important type of management as these managers are responsible for the implementation of the systems that make the company work progressively.

Operation management is about being stable and realistic, with a clear plan for how to develop operations and teams in order to meet projects set by strategic managers.

Management

Strategic managers and operation managers work together to understand what is feasible. They both develop plans for the company and work to create a unified aim.

Strategic managers should not micro-manage an operation manager's decisions. Micromanaging can not only negatively impact the trust in the relationship but neither role will be able to carry out their duties as effectively as they could if they were given full responsibility and accountability for their activities.

Furthermore, strategic managers who micro-manage operations will spend more time analysing day-to-day activities and less time developing business growth plans.

Both strategic and operation managers should be working to develop a brand that is better than the competition both internally and externally.

Externally, the business should be working to develop innovative products/services and a unique selling point that satisfies the customer, while also being socially responsible.

Internally, there should be a company culture and means of operating that is continuously working to develop retentive teams and more efficient operations.

Externally there are many ways to build your brand.

Management

Your marketing message needs to communicate the product's value and unique positioning clearly to customers. Instead of listing the features of the product, you need to communicate what separates your product from the rest by expressing how the product will add value to daily life.

To market the brand and product in a way that resonates with audiences, you need to have defined (or be developing) your goal statement, purpose, and brand promises (strategy document), and provide product features or services that align with these factors.

For example, if one of your brand promises is 'to be affordable to 90% of the working population', make sure you are doing everything you can internally to keep operation costs down (such as investing in automation for time-consuming tasks) so that you can afford to keep product prices down.

Internally you should not only be developing your authentic management skills but should be putting initiatives in place that help improve talent retention. Offering career advancement opportunities, setting up a benefits package, delivering training schemes, and ensuring the workplace supports a work-life balance are key.

The business will also need an internal complaint procedure in place, such as being able to report to various management members whenever a team member has a concern.

Management

For obvious reasons, there needs to be more than one senior member of the business the teams can seek guidance and advice from if needs be. If you only have one manager in place to resolve conflict, what if a team member needs to raise a concern about this manager? To whom can they turn?

A stable strategy (strategy document) the team can understand and get on board with is of significant importance for team retention and building a competitive brand.

A unified understanding of the business direction across each team will reduce the risk of poor decision-making and uncertainty among teams. By having a document of this type, each team can visualise what they are working towards and how the business aims to grow.

Strategic management teams will often see things as simple changes, while operation management teams will know the knock-on effect of the simple changes within the business. For example, opening business telephone lines at weekends.

Strategic management would only be weighing the cost of recruiting more staff vs the opportunity of increased income.

Operation management on the other hand would also be considering the risk of burnout within the management side, as they would be contacted by the recruited staff over the weekend and work would never stop for them.

Do You Possess Both the Integrator Aspect (Operational Management) And the Visionary Aspect (Strategic Management) In the Business?

Different people bring different skills to the table, and it's crucial to understand that a successful business needs a variety of talents. You really need both visionaries and integrators working together.

If you rely too heavily on just one type, you might run into problems, such as launching ideas and products without a clear focus on achieving their main goals or the business could end up jumping from one problem to another without really solving the bigger issues.

Let's take a closer look at these two important roles:

Visionaries:

A visionary is someone who dreams big and can see a clear picture of the future. They're willing to take big risks to start and rapidly grow a business. Visionaries are the ones who can turn an idea into a reality. They're all around us, though sometimes people hide their visionary side because it's seen as unrealistic.

Integrators:

On the other hand, integrators are more practical and stable in their approach. They focus on making gradual improvements to the company over time.

Management

Integrators stick with one thing for a while and work on changing and making it better every week, month, and year. These are the people who build the future step by step.

Integrators often don't get the credit they deserve. Calling someone an integrator and saying they're using "common sense" can actually be a bit of an insult. But the truth is, if being an integrator was really that common, everyone would be able to do it.

In the end, having a good balance of both visionary and integrator skills is key to a successful business. When you create an environment where both types of skills are valued and encouraged, you set the stage for growth and long-term success.

In an ideal scenario, the perfect collaboration emerges when the owner embodies visionary thinking, while operational managers take on the crucial role of integrators. This dynamic partnership forms the very foundation of organisational excellence. Imagine the visionary owner as the innovative architect, sketching bold plans and devising strategies. Their ability to grasp the bigger picture and navigate uncharted terrain serves as a catalyst for innovation, propelling the company to unexplored heights.

In parallel, operational managers, stepping into the integrator role, provide the steady hand required to translate these visionary concepts into reality.

Management

With a pragmatic approach, they meticulously refine and execute the owner's ambitious vision, breaking it down into manageable, actionable steps. In addition to driving positive change, they possess the invaluable skill of shutting down ideas that may not align with the company's overarching goals. This ability to filter out less viable concepts safeguards the organisation from pursuing misguided endeavours and focuses resources on initiatives that truly contribute to its success.

The Right People in the Right Chair

"Right People in the Right Chair" – it's more than talent on paper. New managers need coaching, not just a good CV.

Their past wins don't guarantee future leadership success. Owners often pick managers based on resumes, but thriving in one role doesn't ensure success in another.

As owners, shift focus to coach and back your new management hires.

So, how do we foster these relationships and amplify the potential of our management team?

Clear Goals and Timelines: A structured framework is key. By establishing well-defined goals and a realistic timeline for performance achievement, you set the stage for progress measurement and accountability. This approach guides new managers towards consistent growth.

Management

Creating a Supportive Environment: Embrace an environment that encourages open dialogue. New managers should feel comfortable discussing team-related matters, seeking advice, and sharing their concerns. An atmosphere of transparent communication is a powerful remedy for internal conflicts.

Regular Progress Meetings: Consistency is key. Schedule regular check-ins to monitor progress and provide necessary guidance. These meetings not only keep managers on track but also reinforce their confidence in their role.

The Pitfall of Micromanagement: While oversight is necessary, resist the urge to micromanage. Doing so can stifle team development and hinder task completion. Your goal is to build a self-sufficient team capable of independent action.

Leverage Your Insights: As an owner, your perspective and ideas extend beyond the day-to-day grind. Use this vantage point to identify unexplored opportunities and collaborate with managers to assess their viability. This collaboration fuels innovation.

Empower the Operational Team: Your role is that of an enabler. Equipping your management team with the funds, resources, training, and support they need to succeed in operations is your primary responsibility. This empowerment triggers a sense of ownership and investment in their projects.

The Significance of Quick Hiring and Firing: Striking a Balance for Team Success

The principles of quick hiring and firing can wield profound impacts on the operational dynamics and overall success of a company.

By swiftly responding to staffing needs, businesses can maintain agility in a rapidly changing environment, ensuring that operations continue unhindered.

A new hire's inability to perform optimally or collaborate within a team can be telling signs.

Swiftly recognising and addressing such issues not only prevents prolonged underperformance that might drag down team effectiveness but also upholds the company's commitment to maintaining high standards of productivity and efficiency. More than just a matter of performance, quick firing is a tool for safeguarding the integrity of a company's culture and values. When a new team member does not align with the established ethos, their presence can disrupt the harmony among long-standing team members. Taking prompt action preserves the positive environment that fosters cohesion and shared values.

However, this approach is not without its complexities and potential pitfalls. While quick decisions are crucial, they must be rooted in thoughtful and well-documented considerations. Abrupt dismissals without due process can open doors to legal complications and tarnish the company's reputation.

Management

Striking the balance between swift action and fairness is imperative. Transparent communication about the reasons behind the decision and offering constructive feedback can demonstrate respect for the individual while maintaining ethical standards.

A rigorous assessment of skills, values alignment, and cultural fit during the hiring phase can significantly reduce the likelihood of needing swift dismissals due to poor fit.

Additionally, the principle of coaching and support plays a pivotal role. Offering guidance and training to management hires before considering termination is a gesture that not only respects their potential but also serves as a testament to the company's commitment to employee growth.

In instances where quick firing is deemed necessary, it might be beneficial to involve the broader senior management team in the decision-making process, provided it is appropriate and sensitive. Sharing performance concerns can enhance transparency and help the team understand the rationale behind certain actions, fostering a sense of involvement and trust.

Unified Strategy Process

Referring to the purpose established by managers in the strategy document, as a business you must focus on unifying the why (purpose) across your company.

Management

If your teams are not understanding the reasons why you want to achieve, then they will never fully get behind the idea.

By not understanding, they will be less likely to visualise growth for the company and their role within the business. Visualisation of the goal is necessary to strengthen team retention.

As well as the strategy document, regular reviews (especially with junior talent) to discuss the purpose and how it aligns with the products in development is a quickfire way to keep teams onboard and really establish that need for growth.

Many management teams fall into the trap of simply delegating projects and briefs to team members without explaining the purpose and how it aligns with the activities. Going the extra mile and explaining the why may be more effort but in the long-term, it builds motivated teams and a unified understanding of the business vision.

Good talent will take pride in their work and become invested in the goal.

There's a saying along the lines of 'what you put out is often reflected back at you' and this is true. How can you expect your talent to be passionate about the purpose if they're not receiving the same energy from management?

Management

To put it into perspective, say your business is a training provider whose teams often work to develop student books for different courses.

These projects are often lengthy, taking months of research, writing, and reviewing to complete.

It is important that the management teams regularly check in with the person with this task, reminding them of how the project aligns with the purpose and helps the company reach goals.

For example, the book could be about helping other businesses lead successful product development and your aim as a company is to help products across the world reach their full potential.

By discussing how the book content helps achieve your purpose, your team member can visualise how their work and their role fits into the company for the long term.

Again, your purpose should never be money orientated, instead, it needs to be a statement that embodies innovation or a progressive change.

Once you have established your purpose in your strategy document you should move onto the objectives of the company.

Management

Short Term vs Long Term Thinking

Businesses and their teams are under an incredible amount of pressure to remain focused on the best short-term decisions and earnings year in and year out.

Most people only think about immediate problems and solutions and tend to lose focus of the bigger picture.

Thinking short term all the time is not the most effective, productive, or sustainable decision-making process for a business.

Short-term thinking and decision-making host more risks than one may originally consider.

Example of short-term thinking in Business:

Choosing the cheapest compromises. Price often reflects the quality.

Choosing quick fixes over the most sustainable ones. Consider the impact of a continued and unaddressed weakness within a shipping process. The issue over time may negatively impact time efficiency, brand reputation, and delivery costs.

Jumping into contracts to avoid missed opportunities. Failure to meet demands if unprepared can impact reputation negatively.

Avoiding purchasing assets of value. For example, the building your teams are working in.

Management

You may be worried about owning the building if the business proves unsuccessful, however, by not owning the building you have no control over the rent.

Another example is not wanting to purchase the expensive (but great quality) laptops for your team; when the productivity output drops due to cheap computers crashing and slow loading times, expect a drop in profits too.

Micromanagement. When you micromanage your team because it's easier for you to do the job and get it right, you take away the ability for them to learn the decision-making process, and this can lead to them never perfecting the art of deciding.

Not investing in tools that improve productivity and operations. For example, not developing an app which would improve and quicken customer service operations, only considering short-term cost rather than long-term gain.

A real-time example is when the UK government purchased PPE internationally rather than investing in its own development of a supply chain in the UK.

Another example of short-term thinking is being unwilling to adapt and adjust your operations for different situations/team members.

Management

Say you have a talented team member who regularly expresses their frustrations due to the cost of their childcare, could this team member work remotely and handle their own schedule each week? Maybe they could put remote hours in on a night or work a day on the weekend to help cut these costs and reduce their stress.

Working with your teams to adapt their schedules when priorities like childcare, parent care, and relocation occur will help with talent retention.

These adoptions are especially useful when a team member has been working on an ongoing long-term project; getting someone new in and training them up to replace the current talent because the team member needs to be at home isn't the way it has to be.

Long-term thinking in business means looking further than the next quarter, setting long-term goals for the future state of the business, and making short-term decisions that protect and nurture the long-term goals.

Long-term decision-making involves identifying the potential risks and opportunities that may occur in future and planning the best way to tackle these uncertainties.

It's a challenge to think about the future state of a business when there are so many short-term demands.

However, long-term thinking within your business strategy is essential for many reasons.

Management

Advantages of long-term thinking:

Establishing a long-term purpose/goal for the business that is greater than just profits empower and motivates teams.

Long-term goals help teams stay focused on the activities that matter, to help progress the attainment of the main purpose.

Decision-making is easier with the ability to judge whether an option or business move aligns with and helps achieve goals/purpose/the envisioned future state of the business.

Investing in Research & Development establishes a process in which changes to the market and technology can be identified and adapted.

Research & Development can help with developing unique products and improving your services, which can bring financial benefits to the business by disrupting the market.

Long-term upskilling for teams improves talent retention. Many managers will assume increasing team costs equals a reduction in profits. However, this is a long-term investment that will lower team turnover which inevitably means that teams will spend more time on your business projects, and that your products come to market quicker.

Management

It's important to focus on the skills they need that will help the business become potentially disruptive, for example, digital upskilling. Teams may not realise where their weaknesses lie within their skillset, so it is important for management to keep an eye on performance and industry developments to pinpoint areas of focus.

Development of Management Team

Your role as an owner holds the pivotal responsibility of shaping the future of your business. This responsibility requires proactive engagement and a forward-thinking approach from the very beginning. As an owner, you have a unique vantage point that allows you to foster growth, facilitate better decision-making, and cultivate an environment of collaboration and support.

1. Visionary Leadership and Early Action:

The journey of building a successful business begins with a clear and inspiring vision. As the owner, you are the visionary leader who sets the course and direction for the company. Starting as soon as possible, you must articulate a compelling vision that aligns with your values, goals, and aspirations. This vision serves as a guiding star, motivating your team and stakeholders to work collectively toward a shared future.

Management

2. Cultivating Decision-Making Excellence:

One of your critical roles is to empower your team to make better decisions. Decision-making is the lifeblood of any organisation, and your guidance can make a significant difference. Provide mentorship, resources, and frameworks that encourage analytical thinking, risk assessment, and strategic planning. By fostering a culture of informed decision-making, and actually involving teams in decision making, you equip your team to navigate challenges and seize opportunities effectively.

3. Nurturing a Supportive Environment:

An essential aspect of your role is to create an environment where individuals feel comfortable requesting and receiving support. A culture of support encourages open communication, collaboration, and learning. Emphasise the value of seeking help, sharing insights, and working together to overcome obstacles.

By fostering an atmosphere of mutual assistance, you empower your team to tap into collective wisdom and drive innovation.

4. Leading by Example:

Your actions and behaviours as an owner set the tone for the entire organisation. Demonstrate the qualities you wish to instil in your team members. Show a willingness to learn, adapt, and seek guidance when needed.

By showcasing humility, resilience, and a growth mindset, you inspire your team to embrace continuous improvement and embrace new challenges.

5. Navigating Change and Adaptation:

Developing the future of your business requires navigating the dynamic landscape of change. Embrace flexibility and agility as you steer the organisation toward growth and sustainability. Be prepared to adjust strategies, explore new avenues, and embrace innovation to stay relevant in a rapidly evolving market.

6. Empowering Others to Lead:

Part of developing the future involves nurturing the leadership potential within your team. Identify and develop emerging leaders who can contribute to the long-term success of the business. Provide opportunities for skill development, mentorship, and leadership roles. Empowering others to lead not only strengthens the organisation but also ensures continuity and resilience.

In summary, your role as an owner is impactful in shaping the future of your business. Starting early, you set the tone, direction, and culture that will define the organisation's trajectory. By fostering better decision-making, creating a supportive environment, and leading by example, you empower your team to contribute to the company's growth and success.

Management

As you navigate change and empower emerging leaders, you pave the way for a future marked by innovation, resilience, and achievement. Your dedication and strategic leadership are key drivers of the business.

Development of a Management Structure

The development of a well-defined management structure is essential for effective management within a company. While directors play a vital role in guiding the business's strategic direction, allowing them to become overly involved in day-to-day decisions can lead to micromanagement.

This, in turn, can hinder the development of essential management skills within the operational team. To avoid this scenario, it's crucial to empower the management team and establish clear guidelines for decision-making, particularly in sensitive areas such as customer refunds.

Empowering the Management Team:

Skill Development: Allowing the management team to handle operational decisions, including customer refunds, fosters skill development and autonomy.

It enables team members to grow their expertise and become more effective leaders.

Management

Efficiency: Empowering the management team to make decisions without constant director oversight streamlines the decision-making process. This leads to quicker responses and more efficient operations.

Ownership: When the management team has the authority to make decisions, they take ownership of the outcomes. This sense of responsibility can drive proactive problem-solving and innovation.

Delegation: Freeing directors from micromanaging operational decisions enables them to focus on strategic initiatives that drive business growth and development.

Guidelines for Decision-Making:

Legal and Ethical Considerations: Clearly outlining legal obligations, such as adhering to a 14-day money-back guarantee, ensures that decisions align with regulatory requirements and ethical standards.

Error Resolution: Defining circumstances under which a refund is reasonable—such as acknowledging errors on the company's part—helps guide decision-making and ensures consistent customer service.

Training and Trust: Trusting the management team to handle refunds should be based on their training and competence. This builds confidence in their abilities and encourages responsible decision-making.

Management

Thresholds: Setting monetary thresholds for refunds without requiring director authorisation ensures efficiency and empowers the management team to handle routine cases.

Common-Sense Approach: Encouraging decision-making based on how directors would handle similar situations promotes a cohesive decision-making process and customer-centric approach.

Managing Risks:

Chargebacks and Legal Action: By empowering the management team to handle refunds, you reduce the risk of customers pursuing chargebacks or legal action due to delayed or mishandled refunds.

Reputation Management: Swift and fair refund processes contribute to positive customer experiences and help maintain a positive reputation on review sites and other platforms.

Time Management: Efficient refund handling minimises the risk of spending excessive time and resources on unresolved customer issues.

In conclusion, the development of a management structure for various scenarios, such as handling refunds, that allows operational management to make decisions is crucial for fostering skill development, efficiency, and accountability.

Management

Empowering the management team with clear guidelines for decision-making strikes a balance between autonomy and alignment with legal and ethical considerations.

This approach mitigates risks associated with micromanagement and ensures a more streamlined and effective operational process. Ultimately, empowering your management team to make informed decisions contributes to a cohesive, efficient, and customer-focused organisation.

Develop Confidence in Your Management Team

Developing confidence within the management team as an owner is crucial for the overall success and growth of the business.

Building a confident management team enhances their ability to make effective decisions, take calculated risks, and drive the company forward. Here are some methods to achieve this:

Coaching Instead of Micromanaging:

Instead of dictating every decision, empower your management team by coaching them through the decision-making process. Encourage open communication, provide guidance, and let them take ownership of their decisions. This approach promotes a sense of responsibility and autonomy, fostering confidence in their abilities.

Management

Clear Guidance and Delegation:

Offer clear guidance when delegating decision-making authority. Clearly define the boundaries within which decisions can be made and provide context for each decision. This ensures that your management team understands the limits while still having the freedom to make informed choices.

Teaching Decision-Making Processes:

Educate your management team on effective decision-making processes. Teach them how to assess risks, gather relevant information, analyse potential outcomes, and make informed choices. Provide training on different decision-making models and encourage them to apply these methods in their roles.

Sharing Business Insights:

Provide your management team with comprehensive knowledge about the business, its operations, industry trends, and competitive landscape. When they have a deep understanding of the company's inner workings, they are better equipped to make informed decisions. Regularly update them on key business metrics, financials, and strategic goals.

Management

Ownership of Failures:

Foster a culture where failures are viewed as learning opportunities rather than as personal shortcomings. Emphasise that the entire leadership team, including yourself as the owner, shares the responsibility for decisions and outcomes.

Encourage open discussions about failures and extract lessons that can be applied in the future.

Recognition and Support:

Acknowledge and appreciate the efforts and achievements of your management team. Regularly provide constructive feedback and highlight instances where their decisions positively impacted the business. Publicly recognising their successes boosts their confidence and motivation.

Skill Development:

Invest in ongoing training and skill development for your management team. Provide opportunities for them to enhance their leadership, problem-solving, and communication skills. This not only increases their confidence but also equips them to handle diverse challenges.

Management

Inclusive Decision-Making:

Involve your management team in strategic discussions and decision-making processes. Seek their input and consider their perspectives when making important choices. This inclusivity fosters a sense of ownership and encourages them to take more initiative.

Incremental Responsibility:

Gradually increase the complexity and scope of decisions entrusted to your management team.

As they successfully handle smaller decisions, allow them to tackle more significant challenges. This progressive approach helps build their confidence over time.

Mentorship and Support:

Act as a mentor and provide continuous support to your management team. Be available for guidance, advice, and discussions whenever needed. Sharing your experiences and insights can help them navigate challenges and build confidence.

By implementing these methods, you can develop a confident and capable management team that contributes effectively to the success of your business. You can also implement the use of the decision making matrix, as discussed previously.

Management

Acceptance of Failure and Mistakes

The acceptance of failure and mistakes is a critical aspect of fostering innovation, growth, and a high-performance culture within an organisation. When management teams feel empowered and trusted to take risks, including those that may result in failures or mistakes, it can lead to greater creativity, more ambitious projects, and ultimately, long-term success.

Promotes Innovation: Innovation often involves stepping into the unknown and exploring new ideas.

When management teams feel safe to experiment and take calculated risks, they are more likely to come up with innovative solutions, products, or services. By embracing a culture where failures are seen as learning opportunities rather than condemnations, you create an environment that encourages out-of-the-box thinking.

Encourages Learning and Growth: Failures and mistakes provide invaluable learning experiences. When management teams are allowed to make mistakes, they can gain insights into what went wrong and how to improve.

This culture of continuous learning and improvement enhances the skills and capabilities of the team, ultimately contributing to their professional growth.

Boosts Confidence: Knowing that they have the support of their leaders even in the face of failure can boost the confidence of the management team.

Management

This confidence can translate into greater enthusiasm, better decision-making, and a willingness to pursue challenging projects that have the potential for significant impact.

Fosters Accountability: Accepting failure and mistakes doesn't mean neglecting accountability. It means holding team members responsible for their actions and decisions while also recognising that setbacks are a natural part of the innovation process. When there is trust in the management team's intentions and efforts, they are more likely to take ownership of their mistakes and work collectively to find solutions.

Reduces Fear of Repercussions: A culture that embraces failure reduces the fear of negative consequences for taking risks. When management teams don't fear retribution for failures, they are more likely to take calculated risks and explore uncharted territories, which can lead to breakthroughs and market differentiation.

Drives Adaptability: In rapidly changing business environments, the ability to adapt and pivot is crucial.

An environment where failure is accepted fosters a more adaptable management team that can quickly respond to changing circumstances and adjust strategies as needed.

Management

Attracts and Retains Talent: Top talent is attracted to organisations that value innovation and growth. When prospective employees see that an organisation encourages risk-taking, trust, and accepts failures as part of the process, they are more likely to want to be part of such a dynamic and forward-thinking team.

As an owner/director, one of your primary responsibilities is to act as a shock absorber for the management team. This involves creating a safe and open environment where the management team feels comfortable approaching you with their challenges, concerns, and even failures. Your role is to offer them support and guidance, regardless of whether the failures were a result of external factors or decisions within their control.

When the management team faces challenges or setbacks, your role is to collaborate with them in finding effective solutions. This may involve brainstorming sessions, analysing the situation from different angles, and encouraging creative thinking. By working together, you can help the management team navigate obstacles and identify innovative ways to overcome them.

Your position gives you a unique vantage point to assess the performance of the management team. It's crucial to provide honest feedback about their actions, decisions, and strategies. This feedback can highlight areas where improvements can be made and successes can be celebrated. Constructive criticism is essential for their growth and development.

Management

While being a shock absorber, it's important to strike a balance between support and accountability. If the management team has made mistakes or could have handled situations better, it's your responsibility to address these issues. However, the focus should be on learning from these experiences and improving for the future, rather than assigning blame.

An essential aspect of your role is to foster a culture of reflection and self-improvement within the management team. Help them develop the ability to critically assess their own practices and decisions. Encourage them to analyse both successes and failures to identify patterns, trends, and areas for growth.

By empowering the management team to find solutions within themselves, you enable them to become more self-reliant and adaptable leaders.

Part of being a shock absorber involves acting as a mentor and facilitating the professional development of the management team. Share your own experiences, insights, and lessons learned over your career. Provide guidance on leadership skills, decision-making processes, and effective communication.

By imparting your knowledge, you contribute to the continuous improvement of the management team's capabilities.

Your role as a shock absorber contributes to shaping the overall organisational culture.

Management

When the management team knows they have a supportive leader who values their input and is invested in their growth, it creates a positive and motivating work environment. This, in turn, can enhance teamwork, employee morale, and overall organisational performance.

SAARA Decisions Making Process

The SAARA model for decision-making is a process you should familiarise yourself and your teams with. This process offers tips that will help you and your team make educated decisions.

Step Back from the situation. If you are on the phone and are asked to decide or have an opinion on something, say that you will call them back in 15 minutes once you have fully processed the information.

This gives you the breathing space to think and it stops you from making an immediate decision out of pressure.

Assess the options available. When you first start the reflection and review process, write down the options available and the risks aligned with all options. This will help rule out any no-goes. It is also a clever idea to determine the weight of the decision.

For example, if a decision impacts the future of the business, finances, a client, or you simply can't go back on it once it's made, it's a good idea to inform the person who will be most affected by the decision and get them involved with the process.

Ask For Help, if the decision to be made is an immediate concern or it seems like every option is a poor move, run the situation by a coach, mentor, teammate, or manager. By discussing the situation, you become open to new interpretations and perspectives, and it helps lift the weight of dealing with the situation on your own.

Review the options that are available. At this stage, a review is more than just reflecting on the risks. Take time to ask questions regarding the direction of the business and how each option available supports or impacts the direction.

Action Your Decision, now it's time to put your decision into action, if you get it wrong this time you will learn from the experience and improve your decision-making process for the next.

It's important to remember that if you get the decision wrong, assess whether you could have made the correct decision with the information available at the time, not the information you have today.

We improve our decision-making process by increasing the number of decisions we make. If a change in the situation occurs, then review your decision using the same process.

Management

Building a Trusted Business

There not only needs to be trust within your customer relationships but trust with you and your team.

Trust is a key ingredient in the development of a great and sustainable business.

Examples of how to develop trust within the management team:

Allow the team to handle limited funds, such as a £500 budget card for projects. This not only establishes a level of trust but develops your team's reasoning skills.

This skill strengthens every time they justify purchases to management. It is important not to scorn if you notice an abnormal purchase, even if this is the instinct of many managers and directors.

Allow teams to develop their own project and processes with over-site fortnightly from the management team and directors.

Allow the management team to develop their own projects and process with quarterly oversite from directors.

As an owner, you should also implement these trust-building behaviours:

Management

Be Transparent: Whether you're thinking about changing an operation, bringing in new software, or working through a new concept – share this with your team. Make it open to discussion. This will establish trust by showing your team they are involved in your process and that they have a voice in decision-making.

Show Vulnerability: Being comfortable with sharing your defeats and lessons learned as a manager as well as your wins, not only shows your teams that you're cut from the same cloth, but that they're in an environment that understands mistakes are the learning curve. Nothing shows people you trust them, more than sharing your vulnerable side.

Actively Listen: Be attentive in conversations with your team. This means truly taking in what they say, and not being distracted or pushing your own agenda.

Care: Get to know your team and show that you care. This means learning their names, knowing their interests, recognising their work, saving their phone number, asking questions about their work, and taking the time to get to know them. Be a mentor, not a ruler.

When developing trust in the relationship, there is nothing worse than the dynamic being completely transactional; when the relationship is based on you trusting them to do the work and them trusting you to make payroll, and nothing more.

Management

To have a motivated team that trusts in one another and you as a manager, the dynamic needs to be completely collaborative.

This means hosting regular work events, work reviews, strategy document reviews, daily/weekly 15-minute meetings, establishing team goals, and providing an environment that encourages communication.

Making collaboration a priority, investing in software that allows for smooth teamwork, and establishing an environment that brings people together is the first step in building a trusting and supportive team that cares about each other and reaches business goals.

It is equally as important to be transparent, even when the message you're delivering to your team is not a nice one. This proves that you're not hiding things from your teams and unifies the idea that you're all in it together.

No matter the situation, whether it's a loss in sales or looking to cut costs, talk to your team. When you keep your team out of the loop, they will naturally assume the worst, which isn't good for morale. Honesty helps teams understand why decisions are being made or why situations are changing.

Management

Being transparent and open with team members can help managers alleviate stress and burden by fostering trust and credibility, enhancing communication, eliminating speculation, offering context, soliciting feedback, and giving team members more autonomy to make decisions, resulting in a more motivated, engaged, and productive team.

On the other side of the coin, you can have too much trust with not enough oversite.

Relationship Risks

Even with precautions taken, when you put your trust in people there is always a risk of them misusing it.

For example, when you are supportive of a team member's decision to work from home but then their level of productivity drops, it can be infuriating.

However, there are ways of reducing the risk of foul play in trusting relationships:

Host regular work reviews and set deadlines.

Keep track of your team's to-do lists.

Talk to your teams regularly and pay attention to their attitudes. If it seems like something is bothering a team member, ask how they are.

Bring attention to your limits, for example, issuing a work card with clear limits on spending and what they should not spend the money on.

Management

Have a plan for if financial mismanagement occurs within the company. For example, separate accounts with clear reserves if mismanagement occurs.

Trust & Authentic Leadership

Talented teams by their very nature are driven to progress themselves and the business they are part of. If the business is not moving forward, talented people who strive for growth will leave the business and move on to bigger and better things. That's why, it is important that not only the business environment is trusting, supportive, and driven but that you as a leader are trusting of your teams, supportive of their developments, and driven to progress the business.

Authentic leadership means you are transparent with your plans and purpose, open with your ideas, and honest with your leadership. This is not just a style of leadership, this is who you are.

To be an authentic leader, there are several matters you must understand:

Weakness: You must understand that everything has a weakness. You have weaknesses, your business has weaknesses, as do your products. Do not protest that these areas are perfect when the team are aware they are not.

Core Values: Define your core values, not only for the business but for your leadership approach. Stick to it.

Management

Do not go against your values when the going gets tough.

Core Purpose: Define what being a leader means to you and take actions that align with this purpose. You are a leader to support, encourage, and guide your teams, if your actions do not align with this, then you must review what your problem is and how to improve.

Relationship Purpose: Define the relationship you hope to build with your team and review the actions needed to form this bond and whether you implement them. For example, do you open ideas up to discussion? Do you create strategy documents for your team so that they know what is going on? Do you provide routes for CPD? Are you supportive of their progression?

That's how to be an authentic leader, but what are signs you're unauthentic?

You state to care about team well-being and mental health but allow teams to overwork themselves. Act as a manager when you see teams drowning in work, either prioritise projects of most importance and disregard other projects of less importance for the time being or readdress your work distribution.

You do not pay for breaks, even when your teams must sometimes answer customer calls at this time. Teams who must work during their breaks will become frustrated. Maybe some team members could catch a break from 12-1 and the others could do 1-2 if calls must be answered.

Management

You guilt trip teams when they ask for time off because the workplace is too busy. Maybe you need to recruit part-timers to help handle the workload.

You do not recruit the required number of team members to handle the number of services you offer.

You hire too many new people instead of giving current teams a payrise for taking on more responsibility or investing in automation.

You do not offer teams in junior levels bonuses.

When sales drop you slash the workforce instead of compromising. Instead of laying off teams, reduce hours worked for a short period. This can be hard on teams.

Another example of authentic leadership methods to handle the last point would be to work together as a team to sail through the chopping waters and voice clearly why action is being taken and how it will impact you all (not just your team).

Instead of slashing the workforce, make it known that no talent (including management and directors) will be receiving bonuses this year, and that directorship will not be taking dividends for the next three years. Be careful not to come across as disingenuous here, as you as a director may have received a dividend in the last few months which the management team are aware of. If your business often feels like it's one step forward and two steps back, there may be a problem with your management.

Management

The Importance of Owners

Owners hold a massive influence over the development of businesses. The strategy, start-up operations, growth investments, and business purpose starts with the owner, as does the company's culture. Owners hold a potentially detrimental influence over the company culture.

We're all products of our environment. If a business has a director who is a micro-manager, lacks empathy towards others, overworks, gossips, lacks communication skills, or focuses only ever on short-term profits, it's never a surprise when the company teams develop the same bad habits.

A trusting director who kicks habits such as micromanaging and short-term thinking, and works to develop communication and active listening skills, will inspire the same progressive habits in the company teams.

If the owner inspires a culture of trust through, for example, allowing the team to manage their own operations, it will lead to a unified company mentality of trusting others and taking on personal accountability.

On the other hand, if the directors and management teams micromanage the operations, team members are at risk of slacking in their work and productivity. This is because they know the management team will always be there to pick up the pieces.

Management

Progressive Mindset Development

Cautious managers and teams who run away from taking chances even when they are potentially lucrative need to begin thinking long-term and progressively to grow.

A progressive mentality is an understanding that your business efforts will result in company success. Whether you're currently in an uphill battle or a downhill sprint, it should make no difference to your drive when trying again.

With a progressive mindset, you understand the benefits of iteration. Iteration means approaching challenges and decision-making with an emphasis on continuous improvement and adaption. This means being open to experimentation and seeing failure as an opportunity.

Directors need to be able to see setbacks objectively and recognise the lessons that mistakes can teach them. Failures shouldn't be seen as the end of the line.

Do not allow a mistake to interfere with your company's goals and objectives, even if it results in a brief loss of customers. Instead, concentrate on how you might enhance your offerings to change the circumstance.

Many people tend to ignore the need for resilience and grit under trying circumstances but it's critical when setting yourself up for success to be ready for challenges.

Management

If you want to succeed in business, you must be able to handle conflict by using negotiating and compromising techniques to find solutions. You must also develop your ability to connect with others and enlist their support in your endeavours. You may make mistakes because of this, but you should aim to learn from them.

People without a progressive mentality are frequently afraid to take chances because they anticipate failing. Instead, growth-oriented business owners are aware of the inherent risk in their industry and are equipped to manage it.

You will be able to concentrate on the result rather than the production process once you adopt a progressive growth mindset.

Stretch Theory is the idea that businesses and teams can achieve more by setting ambitious goals that are beyond their current capabilities and must be worked hard for to achieve.

Stretch Theory and a progressive mindset are both related to the belief in and pursuit of growth and improvement.

The focus is continuous learning and improvement rather than being restricted by current abilities or capacities. By combining a progressive mindset with Stretch Theory, businesses can achieve higher levels of fulfilment by making every effort to reach their full potential.

Management

Running a Business vs Working in One

If you as a director are managing most of the daily operations and processes in your business, you are stifling your own business growth.

You will never make the time to develop new and needed products or features if you are always focused on the next task, be it reviewing people's work or answering emails.

Your operation manager or senior management team should be learning the skills to handle the daily operations, but that's not possible if you take it upon yourself to manage all operations.

In essence, your responsibility should be to develop other people within their roles, to train your teams to be able to run operations daily and to give them the tools to do so efficiently.

Your role as a director should be revolving around:

Coaching the operation managers.

Assisting in the development of strategy documents.

Assisting in the development of tax planning and account management.

Managing and supporting the development of profitability routes, revenue streams, and new products.

Assisting new management in developing their leadership and decision-making process.

Management

Recruiting and training a great operations management team.

This also applies to those directors who are self-employed, especially in trade.

You must develop a team to work with you, otherwise, when the day comes in which you can no longer work, you will have no source of income.

This would have been avoided if you put a team together to handle operations when you are not around.

Improving Company Culture

Going back to the idea of building a better brand and being a better manager, it is important to understand that a company is like a living human being.

If you have one person within the team that is toxic to work with, it can lead to a large infection across the whole team that can take years for you to clear.

One person can change the experience for everyone in the team.

That is why it is important to establish a set of principles and values you stand by as a company.

These principles then need to be shared among your teams and any new starters who join the team.

Management

By having a set of principles and values, it's easy to see who is not aligning with the company and the rest of your team, and then any necessary actions taken can be justified.

We recommend you create a culture guide that explains the values and principles you hold within the company, and why they are important.

Below are examples of existing company values to get you thinking about your own:

Support: With the aim of elevating teams and ensuring they understand they are valued. Team events, incentive schemes, and safe channels to deal with conflict help create an inclusive and supportive environment.

Advocate Growth: Learning new things gives people a feeling of accomplishment. Constant learning helps expand team skills, helps improve decision-making, helps boost morale and can improve overall performance.

Equality: We treat everyone in the team with equal respect and dignity. Every team member has equal opportunities, regardless of their background or their lifestyle.

Company culture, behaviour, and attitudes are a component of business that must be nurtured from the start-up stage to growth.

Management

A healthy and supportive company culture is important in the pursuit of success because it can:

Improve morale, leading to team retention.

Improve productivity, by nurturing an environment where teams feel valued.

Improve team collaboration, leading to better decision-making and problem-solving.

Attract more talent, as professionals consider company culture and employee reviews when job-seeking.

Foster growth, by allowing teams to share ideas, make decisions, and take risks without the anxiety of receiving disciplinary when mistakes are made.

It's also important to understand that when it comes to company culture, attitudes can change by how conflicts are handled within the business.

If conflicts are resolved professionally and the parties involved feel supported, teams can maintain trust, collaboration, and a healthy work environment.

However, if conflicts are brushed under the rug and ignored, or are resolved in a way that seems unfair and unprofessional it can build up tension and frustration, reduce morale, and lead to a culture breakdown.

That's why it's important for a company to pay attention to attitudes and maintain an effective internal complaint procedure.

Management

Businesses can approach resolving internal conflict and complaints by following these steps:

Reassure teams that it's okay to express their concerns to management. It's important that management does not react begrudgingly to constructive criticism.

Actively listen to all parties involved before providing an opinion. Avoid taking sides.

Determine possible routes and interactions that may be causing conflict and address any underlying issues.

Work to provide fair solutions, even if this means all parties involved may need to compromise. Guide discussions and keep the conversation professional.

Ensure the solution is implemented and continue to monitor attitudes and the situation.

When a conflict arises in teams it's important for management to maintain a neutral position. It's also important to understand why conflicts occur in teams, typically it's due to conflicting interests and differing perspectives, which is why it's important each party can say their piece.

Below is a breakdown of the steps a company can take to create a healthy and supportive company culture, and prevent conflict from arising:

Establish a set of values and a purpose statement that help guide decision-making and fosters purpose in team activities.

Management

Encourage honest communication among all teams and management levels, to boost transparency and trust in interactions.

Establish clear guidelines, this means defining responsibilities and roles to prevent misunderstandings.

Offer or recommend routes for professional or digital upskilling and CPD training, to ensure teams feel they can achieve more working with the business.

Offer flexible work arrangements, set realistic deadlines, ensure holidays are taken, and limit after-hours work to maintain work-life balance.

Create opportunities, such as review events for teams to meet up and converse, this can help build stronger relationships and shape community.

Reward teams, acknowledge hard work, efforts, and accomplishments.

Implement feedback from teams, address any issues to improve the company culture.

Above all, it's important to lead by example. As a manager, director, or team lead you should demonstrate the behaviour and values you want to see reflected at you, in order to set the tone for the company culture and the rest of the team.

Management

Coaching Role

The owner's coaching role encompasses a wide range of areas where the management team may require guidance and support. By providing expertise, insights, and a fresh perspective, directors contribute to the professional development of the management team and the overall success of the organisation.

Navigating sensitive and complex situations such as redundancy and disciplinary processes requires a deep understanding of legal, ethical, and interpersonal considerations.

Directors can offer coaching and guidance to ensure that the management team handles these situations professionally, ethically, and in compliance with relevant laws and regulations.

Understanding and effectively managing profitability is essential for the success of any business. Directors can provide insights into financial analysis, cost management, pricing strategies, and resource allocation to help the management team make informed decisions that contribute to the company's financial health.

In times of crisis or significant challenges, the management team may benefit from the experience and perspective of the directorship. Directors can offer coaching on crisis management, decision-making under pressure, and communication strategies to effectively address major management issues and maintain organisational stability.

Management

Developing and retaining top talent is crucial for sustained success. Directors can provide coaching on talent acquisition, employee engagement, performance management, succession planning, and creating a positive workplace culture that attracts and retains skilled professionals.

Directors can help the management team develop effective strategic plans that align with the company's long-term goals. This involves coaching on setting priorities, allocating resources, assessing risks, and adapting strategies to changing market conditions.

Introducing new products or services requires careful planning and execution. Directors can offer guidance on market research, product development, launch strategies, and post-launch evaluation, helping the management team maximise the potential for successful product introductions.

Changing Management When Failure Occurs

It's crucial to always keep in mind that humans often have an innate tendency to lean into a crisis. This inclination can pose a particular challenge for exceptionally talented individuals, who often possess a perfectionist streak and dislike encountering failures.

As a business owner, it's imperative that you adopt a broader perspective when issues arise. You should promptly evaluate the situation and determine whether the problem is genuinely significant.

Management

If the problem does indeed stem from a deficiency in your management team's abilities, it might be necessary to implement swift changes to the organisational structure.

The nature of the failure dictates the appropriate course of action:

Urgent Failure: In cases of urgent failure, immediate action is required. This could involve directorship meetings to focus on the issue at hand. The directors may need to visit the site and swiftly devise a plan for change. The timeline for this response should be measured in days, not weeks.

Example Scenario: During the peak tax season, the accounting firm's software crashes, leaving them unable to access client records and complete crucial tax filings.

Example Response: The firm's director immediately halts ongoing meetings and prioritises resolving the software issue. They contact their IT support to diagnose and rectify the problem as quickly as possible. In the meantime, they inform clients of the situation, extend deadlines if necessary, and consider manual alternatives to ensure timely tax submissions.

System Failure with Limited Impact: If a system failure occurs with limited repercussions, it can often be addressed through strategic adjustments. These adjustments might involve making changes to operational routes in order to enhance service quality.

Management

Example Scenario: A minor hardware malfunction occurs in the office server, causing a temporary disruption in accessing archived financial documents.

Response: The director and IT firm assess the situation and determine that the hardware issue has limited impact on ongoing work. They swiftly migrate the affected documents to a backup server while the main server is repaired. Employees are informed of the situation and provided with temporary workarounds to access the necessary files.

Minor Human Failure: When a minor human failure occurs, it's important to resolve the underlying issue and implement backend changes to prevent its recurrence. This entails identifying the root cause and making the necessary adjustments to prevent similar problems in the future.

Example Scenario: An accountant accidentally enters incorrect data into a client's financial statement, leading to a minor discrepancy in reported figures.

Response: The mistake is promptly identified during a routine review process. The involved accountant takes responsibility, corrects the data, and notifies the client about the error along with the corrected figures. The firm conducts a training session on data entry accuracy to prevent similar errors in the future.

Major Human Failure: In the case of a significant human failure, a thorough resolution is required to ensure non-recurrence.

Management

The SAARA framework can be employed to guide the process of analysing the failure and determining an effective resolution strategy.

Example Scenario: A senior accountant fails to meet a critical deadline for filing a client's tax return due to miscommunication with junior staff, resulting in penalties for the client.

Response: The director employs the SAARA framework to address the issue. The senior accountant acknowledges the failure and initiates discussions with the client to assess the impact and penalties incurred. The firm then develops a revised communication protocol and implements stricter deadline monitoring processes. The client is offered assistance in negotiating penalty waivers if applicable.

By recognising these distinct types of failures and their corresponding responses, you can proactively manage crisis, optimise your business's performance, and ensure the continuous growth and success of your enterprise.

Building Management for the Future

Remember, the goal is to shape a management team that isn't just focused on the current survival of the business, but is ready to propel you to new horisons. To achieve this, it's vital to go beyond sharing your current knowledge and teach them everything you know and more.

Management

As you work on developing your management team to lead into the future, it's essential to provide them with a deep understanding of industry intricacies and best practices. This means not only sharing what you know but also expanding their skills and strategic thinking.

Moreover, as the owner of the business, it's imperative to foster a culture of honesty and transparency. Be candid about how the business operates and how the broader business world functions. Discuss the challenges and opportunities that come with it. This kind of open dialogue helps the management team develop a realistic perspective and make informed decisions.

If you find that your expertise falls short of equipping them with the best management methods, consider bringing in a qualified senior management team. Their experience can offer the support needed to ensure our leadership is well-prepared to guide the company's growth.

To sum it up, the aim is to cultivate a leadership group that is geared for the future—a team that not only guides through change but takes it further. By sharing knowledge and strategic insights, you're setting the stage for a management team that excels not just in surviving, but in thriving and steering transformative progress.

Management

As the owner, you have the power to cultivate an environment where the management team can draw inspiration and learn from your experiences. This infusion of expertise can breathe new life into their strategies and decisions.

Here are several key elements that owners can bring to the management team:

Trust and Confidence in Project Development: By instilling trust and faith in the development of new projects, owners provide a stable foundation for the management team to explore innovative ideas and initiatives. This encouragement fosters a sense of security that empowers them to take calculated risks and pursue opportunities. This foundation is only stable within profitable businesses.

Igniting Inspiration for Innovation: Owners can serve as catalysts for new ideas, sparking innovation and creativity within the management team. Sharing success stories, industry insights, and emerging trends can fuel their imagination and drive them to think beyond conventional boundaries.

External Perspective on Business Processes: Often, the operational management team is deeply entrenched in day-to-day activities. Owners, however, can offer an external vantage point that identifies opportunities for streamlining and improving business processes. Their unique perspective can shed light on operational inefficiencies that might otherwise go unnoticed.

Management

Unveiling New Projects and Plans: Owners and directors can introduce fresh perspectives by unveiling new projects and plans that align with the company's growth objectives. These initiatives can invigorate the management team's approach and invigorate their strategic thinking.

Supporting System Enhancements: Improving internal systems is a critical endeavour, and owners can provide constructive assistance through positive reinforcement. By highlighting areas for improvement and identifying potential issues, owners encourage the management team to proactively enhance operational efficiency.

By fostering trust, promoting innovative thinking, offering external viewpoints, and introducing new initiatives, owners contribute to the development of a dynamic and forward-looking management team that propels the company toward its future goals.

How to Manage a Major Crisis

Owners must be quick in identifying an impending legal, financial, and moral crisis that may loom within the company. Each of these presents unique challenges, and a proactive approach is crucial to navigate them effectively.

Legal Crisis: A legal crisis can incur substantial costs, ranging from tens of thousands to millions of pounds. Ignoring or mishandling legal issues can lead to severe financial repercussions, tarnished reputation, and potential legal actions.

Owners must remain vigilant in monitoring legal compliance, addressing potential risks, and seeking expert advice to mitigate the impact of such scenarios.

Financial Crisis: A financial crisis often exhibits early warning signs, which can be detected months before they fully materialise. While some events like pandemics or unforeseen geopolitical shifts such as Brexit can disrupt projections, most financial crises are preceded by indicators that can be tracked. Vigilant financial monitoring, data analysis, and scenario planning are instrumental in preparing for and averting potential financial crises.

Moral Crisis: A moral and financial crisis can intersect, often having a cascading effect. Once employees sense financial instability within the company, they may feel compelled to explore alternative opportunities, triggering a mass departure from the organisation. This departure can adversely affect team dynamics, eroding morale and hindering performance. It becomes a self-perpetuating cycle, wherein decreased performance further deepens the financial crisis, leading to a further decline in morale.

Owners must actively address a moral crisis to mitigate their impact on team dynamics. Open communication, transparent financial discussions, and a proactive response to financial challenges can help maintain trust and motivation within the team.

Management

By fostering a supportive environment, owners can encourage team members to weather challenges together, strengthening cohesion and performance even in the face of adversity.

In essence, recognising and addressing these scenarios demands a multifaceted strategy. Legal diligence, financial foresight, and moral leadership are all essential elements that, when integrated, enable owners to navigate crises effectively and guide the company toward stability and sustainable success. Here are actionable steps owners can take to monitor and identify a crisis before and after they happen:

Before a Crisis:

1. Legal Crisis: Conduct routine legal audits to assess compliance with laws and regulations relevant to your industry. This can uncover potential risks and liabilities.

Establish a strong relationship with legal experts who specialise in your industry. Regular consultations can help identify legal vulnerabilities and provide guidance on preventative measures.

Implement proper document management and retention policies to ensure that all contracts, agreements, and legal documents are up to date and readily accessible.

2. Financial Crisis: Regularly review financial statements, cash flow projections, and key performance indicators to detect any anomalies or unfavourable trends.

Management

Develop various financial scenarios to anticipate potential challenges. Consider factors like market fluctuations, changing consumer behaviour, and external events.

Ensure a diverse customer base and revenue streams to minimise over-reliance on a single source.

3. Moral Crisis: Foster a culture of transparent and open communication within the organisation. Encourage employees to voice concerns or share feedback.

Regularly assess employee engagement levels through surveys, feedback sessions, and one-on-one conversations to gauge overall morale.

Provide leadership training that emphasises ethical decision-making and conflict resolution. Equip managers to address potential moral dilemmas effectively.

After a Crisis:

1. Legal Crisis: Conduct a review of the legal crisis to identify root causes and areas for improvement. Implement corrective actions to prevent recurrence.

Collaborate closely with legal experts to address any legal issues promptly and effectively. Implement measures to rectify any compliance gaps.

2. Financial Crisis: Analyse the impact of the crisis on financial metrics and performance. Use this data to fine-tune future financial projections and scenario planning.

Update contingency plans based on lessons learned from the crisis. Identify strategies to mitigate similar risks in the future.

3. Moral Crisis: After a moral crisis, focus on rebuilding trust and morale. Reiterate the company's commitment to ethical values and create a roadmap for restoring trust within the team. Communicate the steps being taken to prevent a recurrence.

In all cases, consistent monitoring, clear communication, and a proactive approach are key. Engage experts when necessary and encourage a collaborative culture that values prevention and continuous improvement. By implementing these steps, owners can enhance their ability to detect and address potential crises before they escalate and develop a resilient approach to managing them afterward.

Creating a Risk Management Plan

A well-structured risk management plan is essential to safeguard your business's financial health and maintain trust among stakeholders. Here's a breakdown of key risk management measures:

Consider potential scenarios where large sums of money could be stolen from your bank account. Develop protocols to address such incidents swiftly, including communication with financial institutions and legal authorities.

Management

You can prevent such incidents by implementing expense cards for the management team can significantly reduce the risk of mismanagement. This approach enhances accountability, as transactions are tracked and documented, thereby restoring and reinforcing trust.

You can also establish reserve accounts that restrict management's access to the funds. These reserves serve as a safety net in emergencies, providing the company with financial stability without exposing the reserves to potential mismanagement.

Engagement through Incentive Schemes:

One common method of incentivising the management team is through profit sharing. This strategy aligns their interests with the company's financial success, fostering a stronger sense of ownership and commitment.

For companies with assets of £30 million or less, Enterprise Management Incentives (EMIs) offer a compelling way to motivate and reward the management team. This scheme enables the offering of up to £250,000 in share options over a three-year period.

Under EMIs, purchasing shares at or above the market value during the option grant date can exempt you from Income Tax and National Insurance contributions. However, if a discount is provided, you may be subject to some income tax or national insurance.

Additionally, be aware that Capital Gains Tax could apply if you decide to sell the shares.

It is crucial to engage with your accountant or legal team before implementing any incentive scheme, particularly Enterprise Management Incentives. Their expertise will help ensure compliance with tax and legal regulations, providing you with a solid foundation for effective and legally sound incentivisation strategies.

By integrating these risk management measures and incentive schemes, your business can proactively address potential challenges, reinforce accountability, and create a supportive environment that empowers your management team to drive success.

Be Patient With Products

A fundamental aspect of guiding your management team towards success involves fostering the patience required for your product's achievement. To ensure a smooth and effective journey, consider implementing a well-structured timeline that encompasses both the product's launch and its integration into the fabric of your company.

This entails setting clear, realistic targets and timelines that align with the product's complexity and market demands. By providing your management team with achievable goals, you empower them to navigate challenges with a sense of purpose and direction.

Moreover, it's essential to acknowledge that every product requires a certain amount of time to establish its presence and make a lasting impact. Granting an adequate time cushion for the product to gain traction and demonstrate its value is integral to its eventual success.

As a pivotal tool in this process, consider offering coaching and training in agile product development.

Agile methodologies emphasise flexibility, adaptability, and iterative progress, enabling your management team to respond effectively to evolving market dynamics and customer needs. By instilling these principles, you equip your team with the tools to navigate uncertainties and embrace changes throughout the product's lifecycle.

In essence, fostering patience within your management team and providing a structured framework for product development are pivotal steps towards achieving sustained success. By aligning expectations, supporting adaptive strategies, and nurturing an agile mindset, you can enhance your product's trajectory and empower your team to navigate the journey with confidence and foresight.

Patience is critical in the realm of product development for several reasons:

Complexity and Iteration: Developing a product that meets customer needs and achieves its intended objectives is often a complex process.

It requires multiple iterations, adjustments, and refinements based on user feedback, market trends, and technological advancements. Patience allows the team to navigate these intricacies and embrace the iterative nature of development without succumbing to frustration or rushing through crucial stages.

Quality and Excellence: Rushing through product development to meet tight deadlines can compromise the quality and excellence of the final product.

Patiently dedicating time to each phase of development ensures thorough testing, robust problem-solving, and meticulous attention to detail, resulting in a higher-quality end product that truly resonates with customers.

Market Adoption and Impact: The success of a product often hinges on how well it's received by the market. Patience enables the team to refine the product based on early user feedback, ensuring that it addresses genuine pain points and delivers real value. This approach increases the likelihood of positive market adoption and long-term impact.

Resource Allocation and Efficiency: Patience helps in allocating resources judiciously and avoiding hasty decisions that might lead to wasted time, effort, and budget. A patient approach allows for thorough research, planning, and allocation of resources, leading to greater efficiency in the long run.

Adaptation to Change: In today's rapidly evolving business landscape, external factors such as market shifts, technological advancements, and competitive forces can significantly impact product development. Patience empowers the team to adapt to these changes without feeling rushed or compelled to make hasty decisions that might not align with the evolving landscape.

Team Morale and Collaboration: Patiently navigating the product development process fosters a positive team dynamic. Team members are more likely to collaborate effectively, maintain open lines of communication, and approach challenges with a constructive mindset when they are not under constant pressure to rush through tasks.

In essence, patience in product development allows the team to maintain a balanced and strategic approach. It enables them to optimise the product's quality, relevance, and long-term success by embracing the journey's complexities, learning from each iteration, and adapting to the ever-changing business environment.

Taking Small Risks to Develop New Products Without Betting the House on It

In the pursuit of innovation, it's wise to adopt an approach that balances ambition with risk management. Rather than placing all your bets on a single venture, consider the advantages of taking measured steps when launching new products.

Management

Begin with a small-scale endeavour, allowing you to assess the market's response, refine your strategy, and build a foundation of success. Incrementally expand the project's scope as you witness growth in the income generated by the project itself. This gradual approach minimises the potential fallout from a single product's failure and safeguards against overextending your resources.

It's crucial to acknowledge that while venturing into new product territory may be exhilarating, it's not without its risks. Placing all your hopes on a debut product carries heightened risk. If the initial endeavour encounters setbacks or fails to meet expectations, the repercussions can be significant. Confidence, both internally and externally, may wane, making it difficult to regain the trust necessary for future endeavours.

Recognise the interconnected nature of projects within your portfolio. Each project should build upon the lessons learned and successes achieved in previous undertakings. If you opt to tackle your most ambitious project first and encounter a stumble, the ramifications could extend beyond the immediate setback. Team morale, stakeholder faith, and overall project momentum could suffer, hindering your ability to forge ahead.

By methodically advancing from smaller initiatives to more substantial undertakings, you foster a culture of calculated risk-taking.

Management

This approach not only protects against severe setbacks but also nurtures a sense of achievement and resilience within your team. As you fortify you and your team's confidence and accumulate successes over time, you'll be better positioned to pursue larger, more transformative projects with a foundation of experience and a team emboldened by their journey of growth.

Talent

Talent Density

Talent density is the ratio of exceptional talent to adequate talent in a company. Higher talent density leads to a better work environment and consistent delivery of excellent goods and services. To improve talent density, organisations should focus on attracting and developing exceptional individuals while also supporting adequate performers to reach their full potential.

Exceptional talent in a business can manifest in various ways.

These individuals often exhibit outstanding communication skills, expertise in a certain field, or a track record of exceptional performance in their projects.

They possess a drive for learning, demonstrate innovative thinking, and consistently deliver high-quality work.

Exceptional talent tends to possess strong leadership qualities, inspiring and motivating others to excel.

These individuals bring valuable insights and ideas to the table, driving creativity and driving the company forward.

Moreover, they exhibit a growth mindset, continuously seeking opportunities for self-improvement and embracing challenges as learning experiences.

Talent

By recognising and nurturing exceptional talent, businesses can tap into a wealth of capabilities that can propel them to greater heights.

Here are some potential areas of focus for businesses seeking to improve their talent density:

The talent recruitment evaluation process and interviews must be set up in a way that guarantees you will be able to see how well a candidate aligns with the company's culture and roles.

To retain talent, ensure teams have the chance to receive the training they need to excel in their existing positions. Give them clear paths and opportunities to learn along the way so they may prepare for their future responsibilities.

Ensure teams are unified and working towards the company's purpose by communicating the strategy document and setting objectives.

Monitor team performance by paying close attention to individual work output and attitudes.

Talented people strive for workplaces offering continual improvement, therefore, an organisation that places a strong emphasis on continued learning and development would naturally have a higher percentage of exceptional talent.

Talent

Even if your talents are hitting their work goals, you should never avoid dealing with them if they have a pessimistic, negative, or cynical attitude.

To tackle situations like this, ensure that they are aware of how the organisation views these behaviours by having frequent reviews and interactions with them. Give them the space and time they need to alter their process for the better.

Some talent could still be resistant to accepting the issues and improving their behaviour despite all the organisational efforts. If it becomes necessary, let go of challenging team members because they may have a negative impact on the entire team.

Motivation

The level of dedication, enthusiasm, and innovation exhibited by a company's talent while they are at work is known as talent motivation. Since not every task will be engaging, it can be challenging for many businesses to maintain and improve talent motivation. These businesses must therefore discover strategies to maintain team engagement while also monitoring and fostering talent motivation.

Think about a team member that lacks enthusiasm for their task. They're presumably working more slowly, putting off chores, and using their phones excessively.

Talent

This isn't only a waste of your resources; it might also impact other talents, which could prevent the entire organisation from creating work of the greatest quality or accomplishing crucial goals.

Ensuring your teams are motivated is the first step to enhancing talent happiness; by guiding your team with the business vision you can do this. Everyone wants to feel as though their efforts are making progress. What comes after that? What does the company's success look like? Make sure the company's vision is clear because a destination inspires the drive.

Your team will be aware of what needs to be done, but you must go beyond and clarify the why behind each piece of work. Everyone will be more motivated to complete even the simplest tasks if they are aware of how their individual efforts might contribute to the company's larger objectives.

Smaller goals are the key to motivation, even while your business has enormous goals that it wants to achieve. Although each goal should contribute to the broader objective, it feels less daunting to divide it into smaller, more manageable tasks.

Talent will be more motivated to move onto the next set of goals if they consistently accomplish their objectives, which will increase their sense of satisfaction.

Talent

It's important for teams to understand that their managers value their effort. Recognising deserving individuals boosts not only one's own self-worth but also one's enthusiasm and team spirit. It's crucial to provide talent with year-round support, including team-building activities and wellness initiatives.

Time is valuable. Consequently, motivation levels can drastically decline when we do not feel in control of our time and energy. Allowing some independence in the office, whether it be flexible working hours or unrestricted holiday days shows the talent that their bosses have their best interests in mind.

This increases motivation because it gives people a sense of power and freedom to do a task successfully.

Nobody likes to spend their days waiting impatiently for 5 pm in a gloomy office. Talent will look forward to going to work if employers foster a welcoming atmosphere with spaces for relaxation and collaboration. In teams, there is strength in numbers, therefore anyone who is lacking motivation should receive encouragement from people around them.

Talent should be asked what they want out of their careers and given clear instructions on how to achieve them. Planning a career path with team members through growth talks can make them feel motivated to go to the next level.

Talent

Companies frequently ignore well-being when establishing talent reward programmes or motivational techniques. There is no denying that providing incentives like awards can help motivate people, but no matter how hard they try, talent won't perform their best work if they are feeling overwhelmed or exhausted. Giving people's mental, emotional, and physical health equal attention is a great way to keep everyone in good spirits.

Finding a metric to measure talent motivation is challenging. Knowing how talent genuinely feels is the only reliable method to determine this. Some businesses organise frequent one-on-one meetings. You can also ask your team to participate in a confidential pulse survey.

These processes enable you to immediately spot trends in issues before they develop into more serious problems. This allows you to quickly produce a solution, as you can learn what motivates talent and what they perceive as perhaps restraining them. You can also follow up with them frequently to see if anything has changed or improved.

The key to keeping motivation high is to demonstrate your concern, pay attention to their concerns, and take appropriate action.

Talent

Talent Well-Being

Investing in talent well-being can result in improved talent engagement, decreased sick leave, higher performance, and improved levels of productivity. However, because they exist in isolation from daily operations, well-being initiatives frequently fall short of their potential.

Talent well-being priorities need to be rooted throughout an organisation, in its culture, leadership, and talent management, in order to provide meaningful benefits.

Wherever possible businesses should also provide resources for assistance like counselling and health services. Every talent should be encouraged to practice proper self-care, which includes a balanced diet, regular exercise, and adequate rest.

Over the past ten years, there has been an increase in the number of mental health difficulties that have been documented. As a result, there is a rising business need for well-being practices that address both the mental and physical aspects of health and well-being.

The top three advantages of managers putting more emphasis on team well-being is better work-life balance, a culture that is healthier and more inclusive, and higher talent engagement. Organisations shouldn't view health and well-being as an add-on or nice-to-have activity.

Talent

Employers may reap considerable benefits for the health of their organisations if they put talent well-being at the heart of their business strategy and see it as a key source of value creation. To assist companies in reporting on mental health and disability, the UK government has introduced a voluntary reporting framework. This will make it easier to ensure that an employer's strategy for inclusive employment is incorporated throughout the business and taken seriously by management and teams.

Line managers and talent are more likely to participate in health and wellness programmes if they see senior leaders actively partaking in them too, which is why senior managers are important role models. Senior managers have the power to make sure that well-being is a strategic objective that is rooted in the daily activities and culture of the company.

Operation managers are primarily responsible for monitoring the health and well-being of their staff on a daily basis. This entails putting stress management plans into action, recognising early indicators of stress, making helpful changes at work, and cultivating wholesome relationships.

Talent must take responsibility for their own health and well-being as well. They can only benefit from well-being initiatives if they take part in them and care for their own health and well-being outside of the workplace.

Talent

Employers can promote involvement by letting talent know how to take advantage of the resources and perks that are available to them. It's crucial that the company asks for talent input on how to improve its current offering so that it can better shape current efforts and develop new ones.

Engaging and development of staff through trust and accountability.

Training Teams

Currently, employers across the UK are facing a significant challenge, which is the shortage of skilled and experienced professionals. This predicament leaves them with no alternative but to undertake the responsibility of training and nurturing their own talent pool.

When nurturing new talent or training your current teams, there are several essential qualities that you should look for in a person:

- Trustworthiness: One of the fundamental traits you should seek in an individual is trustworthiness. If an individual lacks trustworthiness, it is advisable not to invest time and resources in them. Trust forms the foundation of any successful working relationship, and it is crucial for maintaining a harmonious and productive work environment.

Talent

- Hardworking: You must seek individuals who are willing to put in the necessary effort and go the extra mile to achieve their goals. Hardworking employees not only contribute to their personal growth but also play a pivotal role in the overall success of the organisation.

- Self-reliance: The ability to work independently is highly valued in today's professional landscape. You must look for candidates who can take initiative, make informed decisions, and manage their responsibilities effectively without constant supervision. This self-reliance ensures efficiency and promotes a sense of autonomy within the workforce.

- Teamwork skills: Collaboration and effective communication are vital components of a thriving workplace. You should seek individuals who possess strong teamwork skills and can contribute effectively within a team environment. The ability to collaborate with colleagues, share ideas, and collectively work towards common objectives enhances productivity and fosters a positive work culture.

Talent

Training and nurturing talent within a business play a crucial role in protecting the organisation in several ways:

- Addressing skill gaps: By investing in training and development programs, employers can bridge skill gaps within their workforce. This enables employees to acquire new knowledge, enhance their existing skills, and stay updated with industry advancements.

  A skilled workforce is better equipped to handle challenges, adapt to changing market trends, and deliver high-quality work. This, in turn, safeguards the business's ability to meet customer demands and remain competitive in the market.

- Retaining top performers: Training and nurturing talent demonstrates a commitment to employee growth and development. When employees feel valued and are provided with opportunities to enhance their skills, they are more likely to remain loyal to the organisation. Retaining top performers reduces turnover costs, maintains institutional knowledge within the company, and minimises the disruption caused by frequent recruitment and onboarding processes.

Talent

- Increasing productivity and efficiency: Training programs enhance employees' knowledge and proficiency, enabling them to perform their tasks more effectively. As a result, the organisation can achieve higher levels of productivity, optimise resource utilisation, and deliver better outcomes. Increased efficiency not only protects the business's profitability but also allows it to allocate resources strategically and invest in growth initiatives.

- Promoting innovation and adaptability: Ongoing training and development foster a culture of innovation and adaptability within the workforce.

  By encouraging employees to learn new skills, explore creative solutions, and stay updated with industry trends, businesses can nurture a forward-thinking and agile mindset. This enables the organisation to proactively respond to market changes, embrace new technologies, and seize emerging opportunities, thereby safeguarding its relevance and long-term sustainability.

- Building succession pipelines: Training and nurturing talent also contributes to building robust succession pipelines within the organisation. By identifying high-potential employees and providing them with the necessary training and growth opportunities, businesses can prime future leaders from within. This mitigates the risks associated with leadership gaps and ensures a smooth transition during times of promotions, retirements, or unexpected departures.

Allowing People to Lead

For small companies, it is imperative for owners to grant their management teams the authority and autonomy to lead, spanning from access to financial resources to the space to orchestrate projects that drive the company forward.

Ownership of decision-making and strategic direction is not confined solely to the entrepreneur. It extends to the management team, which plays an instrumental role in charting the course for the business. Granting them the liberty to innovate, allocate resources, and shape projects not only empowers them but also paves the way for a resilient and self-sustaining organisation.

However, as the owner, it's vital to establish clear trust boundaries to ensure that autonomy is exercised responsibly.

Talent

Entrusting management with decision-making authority should not be interpreted as being taken for granted or naively relinquishing control.

Effective communication, periodic check-ins, and defined performance indicators help maintain alignment with overarching goals. This safeguards against potential misuse of autonomy and ensures that the owner's vision and strategic intent remain intact.

Crucially, a small company's survival should not hinge solely upon the owner's presence. A true testament to a business's robustness is its ability to weather storms and flourish even if the owner were to be absent, whether temporarily or indefinitely. This underscores the necessity of cultivating a leadership framework where the management team is poised to steer the ship, making informed decisions and nurturing growth irrespective of the owner's direct involvement.

In essence, embracing a model where management is empowered to lead is pivotal for the longevity and success of small businesses. By entrusting the team with strategic authority, the company not only thrives in the present but also secures its future by fostering a culture of capable, self-reliant leadership that endures beyond any individual's tenure.

OKR

By implementing OKRs, you establish a clear compass that guides your team towards shared goals.

Talent

Objectives encapsulate the overarching aims, while Key Results provide quantifiable metrics that tangibly measure progress and success.

This harmonious interplay between objectives and results ensures that each team member comprehends the broader mission, understands their role within it, and possesses a concrete roadmap to navigate the journey.

Below is how to set your objectives:

Make your objectives Precise, Trackable, Achievable, Relevant, and Timebound:

Precise: Make your objectives precise. If the tasks you define are too broad or generic, the team will struggle to understand the right move to make. They should describe the outcome that is required in a detailed way.

Trackable: By making your objectives trackable you understand whether they are achieved and what impact it has had. To be a trackable objective, it needs to result in either a percentage or some form of feedback. This is also known as quantitative and qualitative data.

Achievable: This means having enough resources and bandwidth to achieve the objective at the time. By not meeting an objective within the timeframe set due to a lack of resources, teams can quickly become demotivated by a sense of defeat even though it is not their fault.

Talent

Relevant: The objective needs to make sense regarding where you presently stand as a business and how it aligns with the purpose.

A completely irrelevant objective to work towards can demotivate and confuse teams. It is important to target the why with these objectives.

Timebound: When will the team start the tasks? When should they aim to finish? Your objectives can be added to the strategy document in the targets section.

An Objectives and Key Results template is a method used for formatting these types of objectives and monitoring team progress.

1st January 2022 - 31st June 2022

Name	Objective	Key Results	Status	Due date
5 STAR Website	Improve website load times	1: Reduce average page load time by 50% in the next 6 months: • Use image compression tools to reduce image file sizes • Reduce the number of HTTP requests by combining multiple files into a single file • Only use plugins that are necessary, and keep them up-to-date • Store frequently-used data in cache to reduce the data that needs to load • Use the loading attribute in HTML to specify whether images should be loaded immediately or lazy loaded	Achieved	24/06/22
5 STAR Website Conversions	Increase website conversion rates	1: Increase the overall website conversion rate by 20% in the next 6 months: • Use A/B testing to try different elements, such as headline copy, images, and call-to-action buttons, and see what has the greatest impact on conversion rates. • Simplify the checkout process, by reducing the number of clicks • Ensure form payment options are secure • Showcase customer testimonials and product demos to demonstrate positive experiences with your website and products	Achieved	24/06/22
Website Security	Improve ALL website security: • 5 Star Courses • Training That Works • QualityMVP • Experienced Crowd	1: Implement SSL encryption on all pages within the next 2 months	Achieved	25/02/22
Moodle Courses Completion	Improve training course completion rate across both platforms: • Mycourses365 • My5starcourses	1: Increase the average course completion rate by 15% within the next 6 months: • Conduct regular surveys to gather feedback from course participants regarding learning materials provided and the tutor training delivery process • Make improvements to the course structure, content, and delivery based on feedback	Achieved	24/06/22
Moodle Courses User Experience	Enhance the learning experience across both platforms: • Mycourses365 • My5starcourses	1: Update and increase the number of quizzes in all courses within the next 6 months 2: Offer personalised plans for learners based on their chosen learning style within the next 6 months	Achieved	24/06/22

Date:

Name	Objective	Key Results	Status	Due date

Talent

Talents Vs Grit

As a director, a key part of your role is to help the management team use their unique talents to motivate their teams toward the company's goals. This means creating an environment where each person's skills and ideas contribute to moving the company forward.

But being a director goes beyond just talent. It also involves having grit. Grit is the determination and resilience needed to face and overcome failures. As a director, you're there to provide guidance and support, especially when things don't go as planned.

In essence, being a director means finding a balance. You encourage the management team to use their strengths to inspire and lead, while also helping them develop the toughness needed to handle tough situations. This ensures that they not only use their talents to guide the company, but also have the strength to handle challenges and grow from them.

As you support your management team, remember that it's important to create an environment where failures are seen as opportunities to learn and improve. Your guidance helps them learn from mistakes and use those lessons to keep moving toward the company's goals.

In short, being a director means combining talents and grit.

By helping the management team blend these qualities, you're giving them the tools they need to inspire, innovate, and lead, all while having the resilience to turn obstacles into stepping stones on the path to success.

Failure Becomes Self-Fulfilling, So Does Success

Failure isn't just one thing—it can take on different meanings. Some people naturally include failure as part of their creative process, embracing it as a learning experience. But the real skill is in using failure as a stepping stone, not a roadblock.

This skill involves creating an environment where failure isn't seen as the end. Instead, thinking of failure as a natural part of the journey helps us become stronger and learn valuable lessons from our mistakes.

When it comes to building a positive work culture and team morale, there's an important idea to keep in mind: Assume Positive Intent. This means approaching discussions about business needs with an open mind. When someone questions a part of a project, instead of assuming they're being negative, ask them to explain their concern. This approach helps everyone work together better, especially when communicating in writing.

Assuming positive intent and embracing failure are two distinct yet interwoven concepts that, when combined, create a powerful synergy for growth and success.

Talent

Assuming positive intent involves approaching discussions and interactions with a mindset of openness and collaboration. It's about giving people the benefit of the doubt, assuming that their intentions are constructive even when they raise questions or concerns. This practice encourages healthy dialogue, prevents misunderstandings, and fosters an atmosphere of trust and teamwork.

On the other hand, embracing failure entails recognising that setbacks and mistakes are an inherent part of any journey. It's about viewing failure as a valuable teacher, a source of learning, and a stepping stone toward improvement. Embracing failure cultivates resilience, encourages experimentation, and ultimately leads to innovative solutions.

By assuming positive intent when discussing failures, you create a safe space for open conversations about what went wrong and why. Rather than assigning blame or dwelling on negativity, team members can focus on understanding the root causes of failure and collectively brainstorming solutions.

Assuming positive intent also softens the emotional impact of failure. Instead of feeling defensive or discouraged, individuals are more likely to approach failure with curiosity and a desire to learn. This shift in perspective enables them to extract valuable insights from the experience and apply those lessons to future endeavours.

Talent

Developing a Coaching Plan for the Management Team

Crafting a strong organisational culture is key for sustained success. This guide offers practical insights for developing a clear coaching plan aimed at enhancing your management team's performance and culture over 1 to 3 years. By empowering your team, promoting open communication, and envisioning a solid future, you can establish a culture that fosters excellence and innovation.

Empower Through Participation: Encourage a sense of ownership and responsibility within your management team by involving them in key decision-making processes. Provide opportunities for their active participation in crafting the company's strategy and engaging in strategy meetings. By incorporating their insights and perspectives, you foster a collaborative environment that values their contributions.

Access to Resources: Grant your management team access to necessary resources and funds for innovative projects. Empower them to champion initiatives that align with the company's vision, thereby reinforcing their motivation to contribute to the organisation's growth.

Aligning Success: Emphasise the symbiotic relationship between the success of the company and the management team.

Talent

Acknowledge that their achievements are integral to the overall accomplishments of the organisation. This understanding serves as a powerful motivator and reinforces a culture of shared success and accountability.

Rewards and Recognition: Demonstrate genuine appreciation for your management team's efforts by regularly celebrating their accomplishments and contributions, highlighting their significance in achieving the company's goals.

Transparency and Trust: Uphold the principles of transparency and trust as cornerstones of your leadership. Commit to honest and open communication, thereby fostering a sense of faith and belief among your management team in your leadership. Never overpromise and under deliver as an owner, and never set goals that are too ambitious for your team to achieve, set regular small goals that can be used as stepping stones to the reaching your company's main goal. This helps keep morale and motivation high.

Accountability and Responsibility: Engage in constructive debates and discussions when pitching ideas to your management team. Emphasise the importance of healthy discourse to evaluate the feasibility of proposed improvements within the operational framework of the business.

Talent

Team Dynamics over Family Dynamics: While building a cohesive management team, recognise that it's not about creating a familial relationship, but rather, a high-performing team. Address any operational shortcomings promptly, either through resolution or necessary personnel changes, to ensure the team remains effective and efficient.

Talent Recruitment and Development: Acknowledge that the recruitment and development of talent rests on the shoulders of the management team. Encourage introspection and learning from any talent mismatches, as these experiences can inform better decision-making in the future.

Future-Proofing the Business: As the owner, your role includes laying a solid foundation for the future. Ensure a sense of security and stability among your team members by envisioning a future for the business that embraces change and technological advancements, such as the integration of AI in operations.

Implementing a Coaching Plan: Developing a clear coaching plan for your management team is a strategic investment that holds the potential to transform your organisation's culture and drive long-term success. By empowering your team, fostering trust and accountability, and envisioning a future built on innovation, you can create a culture that not only endures but thrives amidst the challenges and opportunities of the dynamic business landscape.

Talent

Here's an example of a coaching plan for a management team member that takes into consideration each of these factors:

Empower Through Participation:

Schedule regular strategy meetings involving the management team.

Assign them roles in key decision-making processes.

Encourage them to provide insights and perspectives on company strategy.

Access to Resources:

Provide a budget for innovative projects aligned with the company's vision.

Encourage management to propose and champion initiatives.

Support their resource needs for project implementation.

Aligning Success:

Emphasise the importance of management team's contributions to overall success.

Recognise and celebrate achievements in team meetings.

Highlight how their efforts directly impact the organisation's growth.

Talent

Transparency and Trust:

Share company updates, challenges, and progress.

Provide honest and timely feedback on team and individual performance.

Build trust by sharing challenges and involving them in problem-solving.

Talent Recruitment and Development:

Engage management in the recruitment process, seeking their input.

Conduct periodic talent reviews with managment to identify growth opportunities.

Future-Proofing the Business:

Encourage research on emerging technologies, including AI, to enhance awareness.

Encourage management to explore innovative solutions for future challenges.

Develop a roadmap for integrating technological advancements into operations.

Continuous Improvement:

Conduct regular performance reviews for each member of the management team. This process will provide an opportunity to assess individual and collective achievements, identify areas for growth, and set clear goals for development.

Talent

Use these reviews as a platform for open dialogue and feedback, promoting self-awareness and accountability.

Regularly review and refine the coaching plan based on feedback and outcomes.

Stay attuned to changes in the business landscape and adapt strategies accordingly.

Encourage ongoing learning and development for both yourself and the management team.

By implementing this coaching plan, you as an owner will empower and develop your management team, fostering a culture of collaboration, accountability, and innovation that contributes to the organisation's long-term success.

Marketing

Marketing Strategy & Plan

Creating a marketing strategy and plan is critical for any company. Without either, your customer acquisition and retention efforts are likely to be inconsistent. A marketing strategy is a detailed approach to achieving marketing goals, while a marketing plan is essentially the to-do list that outlines the activities needed to execute the marketing strategy.

The strategy focuses on outlining the target customers and establishing the best route to reach them, while a marketing plan outlines the tasks, budgets, and timeframe to execute the marketing strategy. A typical marketing strategy document involves:

- An analysis of the internal and external factors that impact marketing efforts. These opportunities and risks can be prepared for.

- A definition of the target customers and a clear indication of their needs and wants.

- An overview of the value proposition, essentially how the product is better than competitors and provides a solution.

- An outline of the product, price, place, and promotion.

Marketing

- A marketing budget and timeframe.

- An outline of how to measure the effectiveness of the marketing strategy.

Marketing Strategy Document 02/02/23

Introduction: We are dedicated to offering quality course training for individuals seeking professional development. Our goal is to provide a unique and engaging learning experience that sets us apart from competitors and meets the needs of our target customers' industries. This marketing strategy outlines our approach to promoting and selling our courses.

Analysis of Internal and External Factors:

Internal factors:
- Our brand has a strong reputation for providing quality training and support.
- Our instructors are highly qualified and experienced in their respective fields.
- Our course content is engaging, informative, and up-to-date.

External factors:
- The demand for online learning is growing, providing opportunities for our business to reach a wider audience.
- The market is highly competitive, with many established players offering similar courses.
- Our budget for marketing and advertising is limited, which may limit our reach and impact.

Target Customers: Our target customers are individuals seeking professional growth, including working professionals and recent graduates. These customers are interested in up-skilling, gaining new knowledge and skills, and advancing their careers. Our courses are designed to meet their needs by providing relevant, engaging, and high-quality training.

Value Proposition: Our courses are designed to meet the requirements of the industries for which we produce training. We provide relevant, up-to-date, and practical skill training that is delivered by experienced instructors. Our focus is on practicality and relevance, ensuring that students have the best possible learning experience and are able to achieve their goals.

Product, Price, Place, and Promotion:

Product: Our courses are designed to provide relevant and practical skill training. Our courses focus on quality over quantity.

Price: We aim to strike a balance between affordability (to ensure 90% of the working population can afford our courses) and profitability for our business.

Place: Our courses are delivered online, providing convenient and flexible access for our customers.

Promotion: Our advertising efforts will focus on reaching the target customers through digital channels such as social media and email marketing. We will also participate in relevant networking, graduate, and recruitment events to increase our visibility. We will encourage satisfied customers to refer friends and colleagues by offering incentives.

Marketing Budget and Timeframe: Our marketing budget for the next 12 months is £8,000. This budget will be used to support our digital marketing and advertising efforts, as well as participation in relevant events and workshops. Our marketing efforts will focus on building awareness and engagement with our target customers, with the goal of increasing enrollment in our courses.

Measurement of Effectiveness: We will measure the effectiveness of our marketing strategy by tracking key metrics such as enrollment, course completion rates, and customer satisfaction. We will also regularly review and adjust our approach based on data and feedback from our customers to ensure that our marketing efforts are having the desired impact.

Marketing

Marketing Strategy Document.
Date:

Introduction:

Analysis of Internal and External Factors:

Internal factors:

External factors:

Target Customers:

Value Proposition:

Product, Price, Place, and Promotion:

Product:

Price:

Place:

Promotion:

Marketing Budget and Timeframe:

Measurement of Effectiveness:

Marketing

The marketing plan is a document that describes the precise marketing activities and timeframes a company will use to implement the strategy. The marketing plan includes:

- A description of the company's target market (derived from the strategy).

- A section for channels, how and what you're going to use to connect with your target market.

- A section to define the message, also known as the unique selling point. This is derived from the strategy's value proposition section. This is important to recognise as you and your team need to understand what's different in the way your product/service is delivered.

- The CRM tool to capture leads. This allows you to store contact details and automate certain processes valuable to your sales process.

- The lead nurturing strategy section is the tactics used by the team to keep your leads interested in your business and services.

- The sales conversation strategy section is the tactics used by the team that go above and beyond email campaigns to try and close the sale and turn leads into customers.

- The methods used to deliver great customer service experiences section are the processes you have in place that ensure your customers are happy once the product/service is purchased. For example, a support ticket system that ensures customer enquiries are responded to within an hour.

- The how to increase lifetime customer value section is your retention strategy, for ensuring the business can keep customers coming back and buying. For example, maybe you can implement a feedback model in which you take on customer feedback and use the responses to shape the next developments and improvements for the services you offer.

- The how to develop leads and referrals section discusses the plan for acquiring new customers.

Marketing

A3 One Page Marketing Plan

Companies Target Market: The group of potential customers you aim to sell to.	**Message to target market:** The product/service's unique selling point.	**Channels to acquire leads:** The platforms and methods used to connect with potential customers.
System to capture leads: The CRM tools used to onboard leads.	**Lead nurturing strategy:** Methods used to keep leads interested in your product.	**Sales conversion strategy:** Methods used to convert leads to customers.
Methods used to deliver great customer service experiences: How do you keep customers happy? What services and support are offered?	**How to increase lifetime customer value:** What customer retention strategies are in place? How do you keep customers coming back to you? Are you developing new features, improving customer support, or creating loyalty programs?	**How to develop leads and referrals:** What is the plan for acquiring new customers? Are there referral tactics in place?

Marketing

In other words, marketing plans outline the operational specifics of campaigns, whereas marketing strategies address the overall value proposition, messaging, and the why to inform the plan.

Both documents need to be simple enough so even the most junior members of the team can understand the immediate plan for the company and the why of the business.

If you have no strategy document, then the company will not progress forward at the pace that it needs due to a lack of unified understanding of the brand and product vision across your teams.

Without a strategy to follow your plan may be scattered and inconsistent. This is especially true in small start-up organisations. It is important that everyone within your team understands the marketing strategy to inform educated plans. Having such documents in place and reviewed regularly with your team ensures that it is up to date and that the whole team is on track and understanding how your business is going to progress.

It is important to align the full team with your plan and strategy.

Methods to align your team with strategy and plan documents:

Marketing

● Arrange a quarterly meeting to discuss and agree on changes to the strategy and plan documents.

● Speak to the team about the strategy and plan documents, listen to their suggestions and amend the documents.

● Integrate the Objectives and Key Results template for the team, including the requirements for the strategy document.

● Integrate your purpose within the strategy and involve the team in the purpose to achieve the goals.

● It is important to ensure that the whole team are on board with the strategy before you set off.

Another tool that is useful for planning marketing activities is the Marketing Options Available template, this model allows businesses to visualise the pros and cons of the marketing routes available before committing to marketing efforts. Below is a template to use, and an example of the tool in use.

Marketing Options Available

This canvas ensures you visualise the pros and cons of the marketing routes available before committing to marketing efforts.

Paid Advertising:	Pro:	Con:	Content Driven Distribution:	Pro:	Con:	Platforms:	Pro:	Con:	Other Options:	Pro:	Con:

Marketing Options Available

This canvas ensures you visualise the pros and cons of the marketing routes available before committing to marketing efforts.

Paid Advertising:	Pro:	Con:	Content Driven Distribution:	Pro:	Con:	Platforms:	Pro:	Con:	Other Options:	Pro:	Con:
Search Engine	Customers are looking specially for your products.	Can be more expensive if you have limited conversion. Or if your product is very cheap.	Podcasts	Can be started as a side hustle until you have audience (tribe).	Requires a large investment of time with limited return unless you podcast take off.	Ecommerce Sale	No cost in creating sales.	Commission of 30% - up to 45% - Can take a large margin.	Merchandise	Can allow customers to feel a connect with the Brand.	Requires you to have developed a brand for people when you purchase.
Social Media	Can be very low cost to acquire customers.	People may not be looking to buy expensive products.	Books	Can allow you to develop key person status within your sector.	Requires a large investment of time.	Platform for Leads			Event Sponsorship	Very quick to be done.	Can be expensive to gain sponsorship. Also, if one event is popular the price may change.
Ecommerce Advertising	Can be useful to increase sales on Ecommerce Site.	Can be damaging to your margins due to the costs.	Social Media Sites	Can be very low cost for acquiring the customers.	People on social media are not looking for purchasing as part of the browsing.	Lead Creation Services			Branding of Events Owned in House	Control of the event that allows growth to occur.	Very expensive to start and get to Minimum viable Product.
Video Advertising			Video Content	Can allow you to develop an audience and relationship.	Can be challenging to create video content.						
Specialist Press (Print)	Target audience which is specific to products.	One shot if no one is interested.									
National Press (print)	Very Large audience.	One shot if no one is interested.									
Specialist Website	Target audience which is specific to products.	Can be very expensive to advertise.									
National Website	Large audience of consumers.	Not specifically targeted to specific requirements.									

Marketing

Podcasting as a Marketing Tool

Podcast popularity has soared in recent years, with many businesses using podcasting to connect with their target customers and spread brand awareness.

The growth of podcasting is down to an increase in smart speakers and streaming platforms, making it easier for people to engage with topics they are passionate about audibly.

Businesses can use podcasts in various ways for marketing,

- To promote products, services, or events through sponsored content and native advertising.

- To help position themselves as experts or reliable sources in their industry, by discussing relevant topics within a series.

- To co-produce, promote, or spread awareness through partnering with influencers and experts in the industry.

With the right strategy and approach, promoting a podcast can also be fairly straightforward as a business.

Tips for promoting podcasts:

Marketing

- Define the audience and create content that appeals to them and speaks their language.

- Collaborate with influencers and other podcasts in the relevant niche or industry.

- Encourage listeners to share the podcast with their network.

- Create a podcast landing page on the business's website for the convenience of listeners.

- When promoting the podcast, describe the benefits that people will receive from listening.

- Record a number of episodes before launch to fully engage the audience in the topic. A relevant and engaging podcast will always entice people to listen to multiple episodes one after the other.

- Consider paid advertisements. Paid ads can drive traffic to your podcast website. You can promote them through social media or paid search results.

Marketing

- Inform existing customers and leads about the podcast, and consider promoting through email marketing.

- Notify people about the podcast by posting on socials.

When hosting a podcast series, there are ways to separate a great podcast from the standard:

1. Focus on a central idea: Having a focused topic helps the listeners understand the purpose, content, and relevance of the podcast.

2. Play to the audience: This involves understanding the listener's interests, language, and needs, and delivering content that aligns with these factors.

3. Consistent schedules: With consistent release dates, listeners will know when to expect new content and will be more likely to remember to tune in.

4. Apply structure: Maintaining a consistent structure for each episode strengthens familiarity and makes it easier for listeners to engage with the content. A clear structure can also help call attention to key messages.

Businesses may choose podcasting and podcast marketing over traditional marketing methods due to:

- Podcasting helps businesses easily engage their niche audiences.

- Episodes can be hosted on platforms year in and year out, providing ongoing exposure.

- Podcasts allow businesses to track engagement through metrics like downloads and listens.

- Podcasts help businesses build trusted relationships with their audience.

Books as a Marketing Tool

Brand awareness is the ability of customers to recall a brand from memory when they see a specific product, service, logo, or design. Brand awareness is essentially what separates a product from those of the competitor, which is why it is important to have a highly positive brand image. The ways to spread brand awareness include marketing, events, sponsorships, and word of mouth.

A business with high brand awareness and a positive image in the market is more likely to be considered by customers when purchasing a product. Developing a book can be a great way to strengthen image and credibility through brand awareness.

Marketing

Books, when used effectively, can help ensure a business is memorable and trusted in the eyes of customers; colours, imagery, typography, logos, taglines, and of course, quality content are the components that shape reputations in this field.

Developing books is a way to demonstrate expertise in an industry and the act of publishing a book can be seen as a sign of legitimacy, which increases a customer's trust in a business and makes the customer offering more appealing to leads.

By compiling knowledge and experience into books, businesses may gain a devoted following of customers who are eager to learn more and are willing to make a financial investment in the company.

A business can leverage books as a marketing tool to drive sales and promote its products. For instance, a provider of nutrition wellness training could write and sell books on the subject as part of a course offering or use them to create interest in their services.

The long-term goal for a business that develops books is to establish itself as a reputable source of information.

But how does a business ensure its books and branding are memorable?

Marketing

- Offer unique insights and POV: Businesses that offer a fresh perspective and strong opinions in their content that evoke emotions are more likely to be remembered.

- Impactful subjects: Books that address important subjects in the industry, such as challenges or opportunities, are more likely to leave a lasting impression.

- Personality: A book with a distinctive writing style and personality are more likely to be remembered.

A memorable cover design is also important when developing books, focus on:

- Developing a unique cover design that stands out from competitors.

- Using high-quality images and illustrations.

- Using clear typography.

- Using consistent themes and branding across books. The cover should align with the business's overall branding to ensure it is recognisable.

Marketing

Point of View & Category

Point of View (POV):

A company's Point of View (POV) is its unique perspective on product development, marketing, and the problems its products address. It encapsulates the company's vision, values, and intended impact. A well-defined POV guides the company in understanding its target audience, crafting its messaging, and shaping its brand identity. The POV serves as the foundation for innovation, ensuring that products resonate with customers on a deeper level. It can also extend to the company's stance on societal or cultural issues, connecting with customers who share similar values.

Successful POV Examples:

Apple: Apple's POV emphasises a seamless integration of technology into daily life. This vision guided the creation of user-friendly devices and software, positioning Apple as a company that empowers individuals through intuitive technology.

Tesla: Tesla's POV revolves around sustainability and reducing the world's reliance on fossil fuels. By addressing environmental concerns, Tesla positioned itself as a leader in the electric vehicle industry.

Patagonia: Patagonia's POV centers on environmental activism and ethical consumerism. Their commitment to sustainable practices has resonated with customers who share similar values.

When defining the POV, company owners need to consider several key aspects:

Clarity of Purpose: Clearly articulate the core problem your products or services solve. What is the pain point or need you're addressing?

Authenticity: Align your POV with the company's genuine values and mission. Customers can sense inauthenticity, so your POV should reflect your true beliefs.

Audience Understanding: Understand your target audience deeply. What are their aspirations, concerns, and values? Tailor your POV to resonate with them.

Differentiation: Your POV should set you apart from competitors. It should be distinct and show how your approach is unique.

Long-Term Vision: Craft a POV that can stand the test of time. It should be adaptable yet consistent with the company's long-term goals.

Category Creation:

Category creation involves defining a new market category that addresses a previously unrecognised demand or need. This process positions your company as the leader within this newly created space. Category creation doesn't always necessitate a completely new product; it's about framing existing products in a fresh way that captures attention.

Marketing

Successful Category Creation Examples:

Red Bull: Red Bull pioneered the energy drink category by marketing its product not as a beverage but as an energy-enhancing lifestyle. This category creation shifted how consumers perceived energy drinks.

Airbnb: Airbnb redefined the lodging industry by introducing the concept of "home-sharing." This innovative category allowed homeowners to rent out their spaces, creating a new accommodation alternative.

Amazon Web Services (AWS): AWS created the category of cloud computing services, transforming how businesses manage and store data. This offering was a departure from traditional IT solutions.

Key considerations and risks when creating a new category:

Market Education: Introducing a new category requires educating the market about the problem and its solution. This can be resource-intensive and time-consuming.

Customer Receptivity: Not all customers are open to adopting new categories. Early adopters will be crucial in validating your category's value.

Messaging: Your messaging should be clear and easy to understand. Avoid overly technical language that might confuse potential customers.

Marketing

Reputation and Values: When defining a new category, ensure your messaging aligns with your company's values and doesn't risk damaging your reputation or alienating certain audiences.

Ethical Considerations: Be cautious of claims that could be misleading or misinterpreted. Avoid exaggerations or claims that you cannot substantiate.

Sustainability: If your category is related to societal issues like sustainability, ensure your actions match your claims. Greenwashing can lead to backlash.

Synergy between POV and Category:

A well-defined POV and a distinct category creation complement each other. The POV shapes how your category is defined, and the category validates and amplifies your POV. When creating a new market category:

POV Defines the Category: Your company's unique POV helps carve out the boundaries and significance of the new category you're creating.

Category Validates POV: Successfully establishing a new category reinforces your POV's authenticity and uniqueness, giving your brand more credibility.

Alignment and Consistency: Both your POV and category need to align consistently across all aspects of your business – from product development to marketing.

In conclusion, crafting a clear and impactful POV is crucial for guiding your company's direction and messaging. Coupled with category creation, your POV can propel your company to the forefront of a new market space, establishing your brand as a leader and differentiating you from competitors. However, careful consideration of messaging, values, and ethical aspects is essential to avoid potential pitfalls.'

Owner's Role in Crafting the Company POV:

The owner plays a pivotal role in crafting the company's Point of View (POV) as it often stems from their vision, beliefs, and aspirations for the company. The owner's responsibilities include:

Vision Setting: The owner defines the overarching vision of the company, shaping the foundation upon which the POV is built.

Values Identification: Identifying the core values that guide the company's actions, products, and relationships with stakeholders is crucial.

Problem Articulation: The owner understands the market, identifies pressing problems, and articulates how the company's products or services will uniquely address those issues.

Audience Understanding: The owner must understand the target audience deeply, identifying their needs, desires, and pain points to tailor the POV effectively.

Marketing

Differentiation Strategy: The owner should strategise how the POV sets the company apart from competitors, highlighting what makes the company's approach unique.

Long-Term Direction: Crafting a POV that aligns with the company's long-term objectives ensures consistent messaging and actions over time.

Risks of Misalignment:

Loss of Trust: If the company's products, services, or practices don't align with the values stated in the POV, customers and stakeholders can lose trust in the company's authenticity.

Reputation Damage: Misalignment between POV values and actions can damage the company's reputation, leading to negative publicity and customer backlash.

Customer Disengagement: Customers who are drawn to the company's POV may disengage if they perceive hypocrisy or inconsistency.

Employee Discontent: Employees who joined the company based on its stated values may become disillusioned if they witness values not being upheld in practice.

Employee Morale Impact: Employees look to company leadership for guidance. If the owner's actions don't align with the POV, it can lead to employee demotivation.

Marketing

Inconsistent Messaging: If the owner's behaviour contradicts the company's stated values, it can create confusion and inconsistency in messaging.

Cultural Impact: The owner's behaviour sets the tone for the company culture. Misaligned behaviour can undermine efforts to foster a values-driven culture.

Negative Publicity: In today's interconnected world, inconsistencies between the owner's behaviour and the company's values can quickly become public knowledge, resulting in negative publicity.

In summary, the owner is central to crafting the company's POV and must ensure that operations, outputs, and personal behaviour remain aligned with the stated values. Misalignment can lead to reputational damage, loss of trust, and a breakdown in employee and customer engagement. The owner's behaviours should serve as an example of the company's values to create a consistent, authentic, and impactful brand identity.

Narrative

Narrative and storytelling play a crucial role in shaping a company's Point of View (POV) and its marketing efforts. They help convey the company's values, mission, and unique perspective in a way that resonates deeply with audiences. Here's how narrative and story are important for crafting a compelling POV and effective marketing:

Marketing

1. Capturing Attention:

Narratives and stories have the power to captivate and engage audiences. A well-crafted story can draw people in and make them more receptive to the message you're conveying. In the context of your company's POV, a compelling narrative can grab the attention of potential customers and stakeholders, encouraging them to explore further.

2. Emotional Connection:

Stories evoke emotions, and emotions are what drive human decision-making. When your company's POV is shared through a narrative, it becomes more relatable and emotionally resonant. Audiences are more likely to remember and connect with a story that triggers emotions, creating a stronger bond between the company and its stakeholders.

3. Transmitting Values and Beliefs:

Narratives are an effective vehicle for conveying the values, beliefs, and principles that underpin your company's POV. By weaving these elements into a story, you can communicate your stance on important issues and present your company as one with a clear set of guiding principles.

4. Making Abstract Concepts Tangible:

Complex ideas and abstract concepts can be challenging to communicate directly. Stories provide a tangible context that helps audiences grasp these concepts more easily. When your company's POV involves nuanced ideas, a story can simplify and illuminate those concepts.

5. Differentiation and Uniqueness:

Your company's POV likely sets you apart from competitors. Narratives and stories help you showcase this uniqueness by providing real-world examples and scenarios that highlight how your approach differs from others in the industry.

6. Humanising the Brand:

People connect with people, not just products or services. Narratives introduce scenarios that humanise your brand, making it more relatable and approachable. This can foster a sense of familiarity and trust among your audience.

7. Memorable Communication:

Stories are more memorable than dry facts or bullet points. When you communicate your company's POV through a narrative, you're more likely to leave a lasting impression in the minds of your audience.

8. Effective Marketing Strategy:

In marketing, stories create a narrative arc that guides the customer's journey from awareness to consideration and, ultimately, conversion. Stories can be used in various marketing materials, such as advertisements, content marketing, social media posts, and even customer testimonials.

9. Engaging Content:

In the digital age, attention spans are short. Stories provide an effective way to hold attention and keep audiences engaged. By incorporating storytelling into your marketing efforts, you can keep your audience interested and invested in your brand.

10. Virality and Sharing:

Compelling stories have the potential to go viral. When audiences resonate with a story, they're more likely to share it with their networks, effectively expanding your brand's reach and impact.

Incorporating storytelling into your company's POV and marketing strategy can create an impactful narrative that not only communicates your unique perspective but also fosters strong connections with your target audience. By crafting and sharing stories that align with your values and POV, you create an immersive experience that leaves a lasting impression on those who engage with your brand.

Marketing

Storytelling has become vital in the business landscape today due to its unparalleled ability to forge deep connections and engage audiences in an increasingly crowded and digital-centric marketplace.

In an era where information overload is the norm, stories stand out as memorable and relatable vehicles for conveying a company's values, mission, and unique offerings.

Through stories, businesses can humanise their brands, making them more approachable and relatable. Stories provide the emotional context that resonates with customers, creating lasting impressions and fostering brand loyalty.

Moreover, in an interconnected world, stories have the potential to go viral, amplifying brand visibility and impact. In essence, storytelling empowers businesses to transcend transactional interactions and create authentic, enduring relationships with customers, stakeholders, and the broader community, shaping their identity in a way that leaves an indelible mark.

Poor Marketing

Poor marketing can have far-reaching consequences for a business. It can damage brand reputation, lead to missed revenue opportunities, create a public relations crisis, and hinder long-term growth. To mitigate these risks, businesses should prioritise inclusive, consistent, and thoughtful marketing strategies that resonate with their target audience and align with their brand values.

Marketing

From being inconsistent to offensive, here's how each aspect can harm a business:

Non-Inclusive Marketing:

In today's diverse and globalised world, consumers expect brands to embrace inclusivity and represent a wide range of backgrounds, cultures, and identities. Poorly executed marketing that lacks inclusivity can alienate certain segments of the audience, leading to decreased brand loyalty, negative PR, and missed revenue opportunities. Failing to represent diversity can also signal insensitivity or ignorance, damaging the brand's reputation.

Inconsistent Brand Messaging:

Inconsistent marketing messages confuse customers and dilute brand identity. When marketing materials, advertisements, and campaigns lack a coherent theme or voice, customers struggle to understand what the brand stands for and may lose trust. This can result in decreased customer engagement, difficulty in building a loyal customer base, and reduced brand recall.

Offensive Content:

Offensive marketing content, whether unintentional or intentional, can cause severe backlash. In the age of social media, offensive content spreads rapidly and can lead to public relations crises that damage a brand's reputation.

Marketing

Offending a particular group or community can lead to boycotts, negative press, and legal issues, all of which can harm the company's bottom line.

Misaligned Messaging and Product Quality:

If a business's marketing promises do not align with the actual quality of its products or services, customers will be disappointed and feel misled. This can result in high return rates, negative reviews, and diminished brand trust. Dissatisfied customers are more likely to share their negative experiences, further damaging the brand's reputation.

Lack of Clear Value Proposition:

If marketing fails to communicate a clear and compelling value proposition, customers may struggle to understand why they should choose a particular product or service over alternatives. This leads to lost sales opportunities as potential customers move to competitors who better convey their benefits.

Ineffective Targeting:

Poorly targeted marketing wastes resources on reaching the wrong audience. When a business fails to understand its customer base and delivers messages to irrelevant groups, it leads to low conversion rates and inefficient spending of marketing budgets.

Marketing

Inadequate Communication Channels:

Choosing inappropriate communication channels or neglecting to use the right mix of online and offline platforms can limit a brand's reach. A business that relies solely on outdated marketing methods while its target audience is primarily online will miss out on valuable engagement and conversion opportunities.

Lack of Emotional Connection:

Effective marketing often appeals to customers on an emotional level, fostering a connection that goes beyond functional benefits. Poor marketing can fail to create this emotional resonance, resulting in customers not forming strong ties with the brand, making it easier for them to switch to competitors.

Negative Public Perception:

Continual poor marketing efforts can lead to a negative public perception of the brand. This perception can become entrenched over time, making it difficult for the business to change consumer opinions and regain trust.

Utilising the business viability model, strategy documents, marketing tools, and crafting a distinct point of view (POV), proves valuable in overcoming these challenges. Moreover, here are recommendations to enhance marketing and prevent the adverse consequences mentioned earlier:

Marketing

Non-Inclusive Marketing:

Diverse Representation: Ensure your marketing materials reflect a range of demographics, cultures, and identities.

Research and Understanding: Understand your audience's preferences and cultural nuances to avoid inadvertently excluding or offending anyone.

Inclusive Language: Use inclusive language that respects different backgrounds and identities.

Inconsistent Brand Messaging:

Brand Guidelines: Develop clear brand guidelines that outline the brand's tone, voice, and visual identity.

Centralised Approval: Have a centralised approval process to ensure all marketing materials adhere to the established guidelines.

Message Alignment: Ensure that all marketing channels convey a consistent message and brand identity.

Offensive Content:

Marketing Guidelines/Brand Kit: A marketing guideline document is a reference sheet for the team that provides standards, recommendations, and best practices for consistent marketing strategies. It covers brand identity, tone, logo, typography, colours, imagery, messaging, content, social media, advertising, ethics, and legal considerations.

Marketing

It ensures uniformity, simplifies decision-making, and aids in maintaining a cohesive brand image and message across platforms.

Sensitivity Training: Provide training to your team on cultural sensitivity and avoiding offensive content.

User Testing: Test marketing materials with a diverse group of people before launching campaigns.

Misaligned Messaging and Product Quality:

Honest Communication: Ensure that marketing messages accurately reflect the product's features and benefits.

Transparent Reviews: Encourage genuine customer reviews to provide honest feedback on the product's quality.

Quality Control: Maintain consistent product quality to match the promises made in marketing materials.

Lack of Clear Value Proposition:

Customer Insights: Understand your customers' needs and pain points to create a compelling value proposition.

Differentiation: Clearly articulate what sets your product or service apart from competitors.

Visual Communication: Use visuals, videos, and infographics to help explain complex value propositions.

Marketing

Ineffective Targeting:

Audience Research: Conduct thorough audience research to understand their demographics, behaviours, and preferences.

Segmentation: Divide your audience into segments based on shared characteristics for more precise targeting.

Personalisation: Tailor your marketing messages to each audience segment to increase relevance.

Inadequate Communication Channels:

Audience Behaviour: Determine where your target audience spends their time online and offline.

Multichannel Approach: Utilise a mix of channels that your audience prefers, including social media, email, blogs, and events.

Analytics: Monitor the performance of different channels to refine your strategy over time.

Lack of Emotional Connection:

Storytelling: Use storytelling to create emotional connections by highlighting customer success stories or the brand's journey.

Values Alignment: Showcase the brand's values and how they align with customer beliefs and aspirations.

Marketing

Empathy: Show understanding and empathy toward customer challenges to build a rapport.

Negative Public Perception:

Rebranding or Repositioning: If necessary, consider rebranding or repositioning your brand to change public perception.

Transparent Communication: Address negative perceptions openly and provide solutions or improvements.

Consistency and Patience: Consistently deliver on promises and engage in long-term efforts to rebuild trust.

CAC

Managing Customer Acquisition Costs (CAC) is a crucial aspect of any business strategy, and ensuring that CAC is not higher than the customer's lifetime value (CLV) is essential for long-term profitability and sustainable growth. Here's why this principle is important:

Profitability: The fundamental goal of any business is to generate profit. If your CAC exceeds the CLV, it means you're spending more to acquire customers than you'll earn from them over their relationship with your business. This erodes profitability and can lead to financial instability.

Sustainability: Maintaining a healthy CAC-to-CLV ratio is essential for the long-term sustainability of your business. If you consistently spend more to acquire customers than they generate in revenue, your business model isn't viable in the long run. This can lead to financial troubles and potential business failure.

Resource Allocation: Efficiently managing CAC helps you allocate your resources effectively. Overspending on customer acquisition could mean you have fewer resources available for product development, customer support, and other areas that contribute to overall customer satisfaction and loyalty.

Maximising ROI: Keeping CAC in check relative to CLV ensures that your return on investment (ROI) remains positive. You want to make sure that the money you invest in acquiring customers generates more revenue than you've spent, leading to a higher ROI and better overall financial performance.

Customer Lifetime Value: Focusing solely on acquiring new customers without considering their lifetime value can result in missed opportunities. Repeat customers tend to spend more over time and can become brand advocates, referring new customers to your business. If your CAC is too high, you might miss out on these benefits.

Reducing Churn: When your CAC is aligned with CLV, you're incentivised to keep your customers engaged and satisfied for the long term. This can lead to better customer retention rates, reducing churn and saving on the costs associated with constantly replacing lost customers.

Market Competition: In competitive markets, customers have more choices. If your CAC exceeds what customers are worth to you, it becomes difficult to compete effectively on price and offer attractive deals to potential customers.

Risk Management: A high CAC relative to CLV introduces financial risk. Economic downturns, changes in consumer behaviour, or shifts in your industry can impact customer acquisition costs. If you're already operating with a narrow margin, these external factors can have a disproportionate negative impact on your business.

Strategic Decision-Making: The CAC-to-CLV ratio influences strategic decisions such as pricing, marketing budget allocation, and customer segmentation. Businesses need to strike a balance between investing in acquisition and retaining existing customers, and this balance is informed by the CAC-to-CLV relationship.

In conclusion, managing CAC to ensure it doesn't exceed the customer's lifetime value is crucial for building a sustainable, profitable, and growth-oriented business. This requires careful analysis, continuous monitoring, and a holistic understanding of your customers' behaviour and value to your business.

Monitoring Leads

Monitoring the quantity and quality of leads is essential for the success of any business. Leads are the potential customers who have shown interest in your products or services, and ensuring a steady flow of leads can have a significant impact on your business's growth and profitability. Here's why monitoring lead generation is important:

Business Growth: Leads are the foundation of your customer base. Without a consistent influx of new leads, your business can stagnate or decline over time. A steady stream of leads provides the opportunity to convert more customers and expand your market share.

Sales Conversion: Not all leads are equal in terms of their readiness to purchase. Monitoring lead quality helps you focus your resources on leads that are more likely to convert into paying customers. This leads to a higher conversion rate and a more efficient sales process.

Marketing

Optimising Marketing Efforts: Tracking lead sources and conversion rates allows you to identify which marketing channels and campaigns are most effective. This data-driven approach enables you to allocate your marketing budget more effectively and refine your strategies for maximum impact.

Customer Insights: Monitoring leads provides insights into customer behaviour, preferences, and pain points. Understanding your leads' needs can inform product development, marketing messaging, and customer service improvements.

Sales Forecasting: Predictable lead generation allows for more accurate sales forecasting. This is crucial for setting realistic goals, managing inventory, and planning for periods of high demand.

Continuous Improvement: Regularly monitoring lead generation metrics helps you identify trends and patterns. By analysing this data, you can make informed adjustments to your marketing strategies, messaging, and targeting for better results over time.

Adapting to Changes: Market dynamics, consumer preferences, and technology evolve over time. Monitoring leads allows you to adapt to these changes more effectively and adjust your strategies to remain relevant and competitive.

Cost Efficiency: Generating high-quality leads is generally more cost-effective than broad, indiscriminate marketing efforts. Monitoring leads helps you identify the most cost-efficient channels and tactics, maximising your marketing ROI.

In summary, monitoring lead generation is a crucial practice for businesses of all sizes. It enables you to optimise your marketing efforts, convert more customers, and drive business growth. By understanding where your leads come from, how they behave, and what they need, you can make informed decisions that contribute to the overall success of your business.

Steps to monitor leads effectively:

Define Metrics: Choose key lead generation metrics (e.g., website visits, form submissions, conversion rates).

Use Tools: Utilise CRM systems, analytics platforms, and marketing automation tools.

Segment Leads: Categorise leads based on behaviour and engagement level.

Analyse Sources: Identify where leads originate (e.g., social media, website, referrals).

Conversion Tracking: Track leads' journey from initial contact to conversion.

Regular Analysis: Regularly review data to identify trends and patterns.

A/B Testing: Experiment with different strategies and measure their impact.

Refine Strategies: Adapt tactics based on insights to improve lead quality.

Feedback Loop: Collaborate with sales teams to gather feedback on lead quality.

Continuous Improvement: Make data-driven adjustments to enhance lead generation.

Understanding Customer Acquisition Cost (CAC) and Customer Lifetime Value (CLV) is equally crucial for effective lead monitoring. These concepts provide valuable insights into the financial and strategic aspects of your lead generation efforts.

Lead Quality Assessment: By linking CAC and CLV to lead quality, you can evaluate whether the cost of acquiring leads aligns with their potential lifetime value.

Segmentation and Targeting: Analysing CAC and CLV alongside lead behaviour can guide you in refining your targeting strategies. You can attract leads with characteristics similar to high CLV customers while keeping CAC in check.

Marketing

Conversion Optimisation: Understanding CAC helps you optimise conversion strategies, ensuring that the costs associated with converting leads remain reasonable compared to the expected returns.

Performance Benchmarking: Comparing CAC to CLV benchmarks can give you insights into how efficiently you're converting leads into valuable, long-term customers.

In essence, CAC and CLV provide financial context to your lead monitoring efforts. They enable you to make informed decisions about where to invest, which leads to prioritise, and how to tailor your strategies for maximum profitability and sustainable growth.

Marketing Challenges

Marketing can be a key player in business growth, enabling companies to connect with their target audience, build brand recognition, and drive sales.

However, like any business endeavour, marketing comes with its own set of challenges and uncertainties, including the potential for various cost risks.

As organisations invest resources into advertising campaigns, promotional activities, and brand-building efforts, it's crucial to understand and navigate the potential financial pitfalls that can impact the bottom line.

Marketing

One of the most significant cost risks in marketing is the uncertainty of ROI. Not all marketing efforts yield immediate or proportional returns. Businesses might invest heavily in campaigns, advertising, or promotional activities without a guarantee of positive outcomes. This uncertainty can lead to inefficient allocation of resources and wasted budget.

Without careful budget planning and monitoring, marketing expenses can quickly spiral out of control. Overspending on marketing initiatives can strain finances and lead to reduced profitability. It's crucial to establish a budget and stick to it while continuously evaluating the effectiveness of spending.

Implementing marketing strategies that don't resonate with the target audience can be costly. If a campaign's messaging or channels fail to connect with customers, the money invested in these efforts can go to waste.

Without proper tracking and analytics, it's challenging to measure the effectiveness of marketing efforts. Businesses might continue investing in campaigns that aren't delivering results because they lack the data to make informed decisions.

To mitigate these cost risks, business owners should adopt a strategic approach to marketing that involves thorough research, data-driven decision-making, regular performance evaluations, and a willingness to adapt strategies based on real-time feedback.

Marketing

Diversifying marketing efforts, setting clear objectives, and aligning marketing activities with overall business goals can help minimise the financial challenges associated with marketing endeavours.

Neglecting to recognise the potential cost risks in marketing can lead to serious problems for a business. This includes wasting resources on ineffective strategies, overspending without good returns, missing chances for growth, damaging the brand's reputation, and causing financial strain. The business could also struggle to keep up with changes in the market, resulting in inconsistent messaging and eventual stagnation.

The role of an owner is pivotal for orchestrating success. The BAMTM framework empowers owners to cultivate productivity, fortify foundations for powering through challenges, and propel businesses to unparalleled heights.

Conclusion

Incorporating the BAMTM framework leads companies toward streamlined operations and wise decision-making. It is up to you as the reader to continue implementing the practices taught in this guide to unleash your company's potential for success. It's important to remember that success doesn't happen overnight, and it takes time, effort, and consistency to see results.

A productive business that implements the practices taught and continuously works to improve its infrastructure and customer offering will foster opportunities for increased profits, growth and expansion, improved reputation and customer satisfaction, and job creation.

If more businesses in the UK continuously worked to improve their operations and customer offering, it would have a positive impact on the standard of living and economy. Improved operations would lead to more efficient and cost-effective businesses, which would drive competition and result in better products and services for customers.

This, in turn, would increase customer confidence and spending, which would drive economic growth. Additionally, a more dynamic and competitive business environment will attract more investment and create more jobs, further boosting the economy and standard of living. As a business, don't settle for mediocrity - take the first steps towards sustainable success with BAMTM.